I Can't Believe It's Not Better

M O N I C A   H E I S E Y

Red Deer Press

For my parents. Thank you for everything and sorry about all the goddamn swears.

Published in Canada by Red Deer Press, 195 Allstate Parkway, Markham, Ontario L3R 4T8

Published in the United States by Red Deer Press, 311 Washington Street, Brighton, Massachusetts 02135

www.reddeerpress.com

10 9 8 7 6 5 4 3 2 1

Some material included was first published and adapted from "The Grown Ass Woman's Guide by Monica Heisey," a column on Shedoesthecity.com, between 2012 and 2014.

Red Deer Press acknowledges with thanks the Canada Council for the Arts, and the Ontario Arts Council for their support of our publishing program. We acknowledge the financial support of the Government of Canada through the Canada Book Fund (CBF) for our publishing activities.

Library and Archives Canada Cataloguing in Publication
Heisey, Monica, author
    I can't believe it's not better : a woman's guide to coping with life / Monica Heisey.
ISBN 978-0-88995-535-6 (pbk.)
    I. Title.
PS8375.H44 2015   C818'.602   C2015-902242-8

Publisher Cataloging-in-Publication Data (U.S.)
Heisey, Monica, author
    I can't believe it's not better : a woman's guide to coping with life
/ Monica Heisey.
ISBN 978-0-88995-535-6
Data available on file.

Cover design by Jenn Kitagawa
Text design by Kong Njo
Printed in Canada by Friesens Corporation

Contents

"Our Modern World" 207

An Introduction

Hi! I'm so excited you're here. I just hope I brought enough jokes about chips for everyone. I know what you're thinking: "Who is this beautiful genius?" "Are there really going to be chips?" and "Honestly I can tell she's beautiful just from reading her prose, which sounds crazy but nothing has ever felt more real." Well. My name is Monica Heisey (as you probably saw on the front of the book, but hello again) and I am very excited to be here. I am especially excited to be here because I did not really think I would get to write this or any book, at least not right now. I am not a television personality, or an heiress, or even that most dubious of claims, a "social media celebrity." I am just a girl, standing in front of a book, asking you to love it.

Actually, I am a comedian and writer from Canada who in 1998 wrote a short story called "The James Bond School For Girls," about a secret preteen spy academy where "geekiness was next to godliness." I know what you're thinking again: "That's very sad. I'm sad right now." Me too. Life is hard. Still, I suppose it is important that we get to know each other before embarking on this textual "Odyssey of the Mind," so here are some other things you should know about me:

- "Odyssey of the Mind" is the name of an elementary school history competition I participated in as a Young Nerd (also in 1998) (it was a big year for me). My team put together a play that answered the important historical question, "What if Shakespeare and Copernicus were friends?" We did not win.
- I recently spent almost five years living in London, UK. I spent exactly this amount of time struggling not to buy a cape.
- I now live in Toronto, where my sartorial struggles are humbler and largely weather-based.
- In university a roommate once moved out of my house under the cover of night, leaving only a Pussycat Dolls poster and a used sanitary pad in a half-eaten container of poutine. A Canadian tragedy if there ever was one (all that wasted poutine!).
- I am probably 8.7—9 out of 10 in terms of sex, depending on the day.
- Once, at a dentist appointment, the dentist poked at the roof of my mouth, looked at me knowingly and said, "Pizza burns?" in a very sympathetic tone.

I mean, that's basically everything. All the important cape facts are there. To this I would only add that I have a very nice family with a mom and a dad and a twin sister and a baby sister and a weird old dog and a li'l cat and a tall boyfriend. I consider dairy a personal friend and am technically allergic to the sun; I will never stop trying to make hats work for me. (It's an uphill battle, but one I am dedicated to winning.) I am interested in female friendship, strategies for effectively working from home, the science behind Investment Bras and why some people choose to spell it "kewl" when it is the same number of letters as the real word and actually more effort to type because you have to press all different keys instead of two Os. I want to help you eat in bed effectively and text back within the right timeframe and take perfect selfies and split the cheque without your cheapest friend getting mad.

So the book you are holding deals with some of that stuff, but mostly it deals with the stuff of being alive and embarrassed and trying to do better or at least enjoy yourself. It deals especially with doing the above while female and youngish, because those are things that I am, but it is my hope that there's something useful or at least amusing in here for everyone. While, tragically, my 1998 James Bond sadness fantasy did not make it into this volume, the book is packed with life advice, some home truths, and a story about the time I barfed on a Heathrow airport customs official. Inside, if you read carefully, you will also learn:

- where to go to cry in public.
- whether or not you are currently being flirted with.
- when it's time to switch to water (hint: right around "Jill, are you mad at me? No, Jill... JILL. Are you?").
- some difficult workplace truths for filthy, unemployable Millennials.
- what to call your boyfriend or girlfriend (hint: not "lover").
- all the ways my body is being sneaky right now.
- how to make your apartment look like you read design blogs (hint: jars).
- what it might look like if the bat signal was for butts, i.e. a "butt signal."
- more about dips than you probably care to know.

XII ♦ I Can't Believe It's Not Better

- why all women know what fruit their body is shaped like (hint: the patriarchy).

And between twelve and sixteen other things, depending on how much you're bringing to this reading experience. The helpful hints, informative quizzes and bizarre, burrito-heavy anecdotes that make up this work come mostly from my lived experience, and occasionally from the frightening nightmare world that is my imagination. They are poems and short stories, advice columns and sketches and essays and lists, and they all exist to help me and you figure out a few things about this weird little life. I have endeavoured to pass along some knowledge, yes, but mostly, to be honest, I'd like to make you laugh. You may have noticed some jokes in the above paragraphs, and keep your eyes peeled: there are four or five more where that came from. The astute comic eye may note as many as seven full "bits."

One of the best things about being a comedian is that everyone around you is incredibly generous with their own comic material. They're just giving this stuff away! The sheer number of free dick jokes, sexist premises, and sketches about the way waiters talk to you when you're over fifty I've been given over the years is mind-boggling. Below are some jokes I was told I could "have" for the book:

- a bit about how difficult it is to remember all your different Internet passwords.
- "what if tampons were for guys."
- a long interlude about the difference between 90s kids and children of the 80s.
- "what if a bra kept a diary."

- something I'll just call "salad humour."
- "how do you spell Dad? C-O-O-L."

Please see page 172 for "Diary of A Bra." Please see my forthcoming series *Jokes My Dad Suggested I Use In My Professional Comedy Career* Vols. 1 through 87 for that fun "Dad = Cool" riff (and much, much more!). And for the best I can offer in terms of what to do with your life, please see this book.

WE ARE ALL IN THE GUTTER
BUT SOME OF US

ARE MAKING OUT WITH OTHER
PEOPLE FROM THE GUTTER.

1

FOOD

A Factual And Emotional History Of The Burrito

The end of my life's first great love occurred within moments of discovering my second. This will perhaps sound less callous when I note that my life's second great love affair has been with burritos. There have been new relationships since that first love of course, but they've all been either equal or secondary to my relationship with some combination of refried beans, cheese, guacamole, and tortilla.

* * *

The word burrito means "little donkey." The reason for this is unknown. The most popular theory is that it was served out of the back of donkey carts. Certainly donkey has never been an ingredient. Some theories suggest burritos look like the bed rolls donkeys often carried, and more creative types have suggested they look like donkey's ears... to be honest everyone seems to be dancing around the "little donkey" idea without much guidance.

* * *

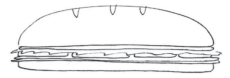

SUBTWEET (noun):

When you tweet something
kind of vague but everyone
knows it's about a sandwich.

Paul and I met at university. He was part-Mexican, as he told me often. He was very proud of this. The purported ratio of Mexican to non-Mexican parts was unclear, and shifted throughout the course of our relationship as I met more and more of his family members who turned out not to be Mexican at all. He was 50/50 until I met his parents, a Scottish-Canadian man named, literally, William Blake, and a blonde woman with a gap in her teeth that she claimed was lucky. Paul hovered around twenty-five percent until I met his grandmother, who had in fact been born in Mexico, but had run away to Canada with her European high school teacher at eighteen. In the end, I think we settled on one-eighth. Yet somehow, from our first meal together in the autumn of 2006 to our second-last in the fall of 2009, we did not consume a single burrito.

•••

Mexico does not actually consume that many burritos per year. While the dish is traditional to some areas in the north, in the south of Mexico it exists almost exclusively for tourists. What you think of when you picture a burrito is basically an impostor food.

•••

Burritos are, I think, the perfect comfort food. Warm and soft and filling, a light crunch provided by lettuce and some vegetables to complement the overall oozy texture of guacamole, beans, melted cheese, and sour cream. The kind of thing you can't really eat alone. Someone needs to be there, a testament to the fact that a burrito is a choice you are making, not a lifestyle. You have friends and a job and a life outside of this dimly-lit restaurant with the linoleum floor and the folding chairs, and you will return to it shortly, but first you will do something truly unspeakable to the foil-wrapped parcel in front of you containing enough food to reasonably feed three full-sized adult humans.

The Diccionario de Mexicanismos *has an entry for the burrito dating as early as 1895. It states that a burrito is "a rolled tortilla with meat or other ingredients inside, called 'coçito' in Yucatán and 'taco' in the city of Cuernavaca and in Mexico City." There is some suggestion that burritos are a war food, brought into America during the Mexican/American strife of the early 1900s. There is very little written documentation of the burrito's early days. Presumably all surrounding paper was used as napkins.*

Paul and I met at a house party. A friend of mine in first-year was dating a guy who was—if you can believe it—in second. He had his own house and we could. Not. Stand it. They were throwing a back-to-school party and we (young, eager freshman that we were) got there embarrassingly early. So early that when a tall, handsome, partially Mexican man answered the door, he was not yet wearing a shirt. He had a six pack. (This mattered, at the time. I was still being weaned off Josh Hartnett posters ripped out of *YM*.) The six pack later told me that his name was Paul. And that he was shirtless because "all" of his clothes were in the wash. We found we shared a drama class and made a habit of having lunch together afterwards. When I went on a few dates with one of his friends, he made fun of me. One night we had planned to meet friends at a local club, in the middle of the gross Canadian winter. Everyone cancelled. "Should we still go?" he asked. "Sure."

* *

The first mention of a burrito in the Los Angeles Times *wasn't until 1958, the same year the term initially appeared in the* Oxford English Dictionary. *The almost sixty years of silence between the* Diccionario *reference and these references were hopefully the work of an Illuminati-style secret gang with delicious but nefarious intentions.*

* *

The morning after that whiskey sour-drenched night we made breakfast and I wore his sweatpants. We annoyed our friends for the rest of the semester, and presumably several years beyond. Through some teen romance voodoo we spent the summer in Italy, living and working in a dried-up ski town in the Alps for a now-defunct government program that took bureaucrats' children away from them while they weren't in school. We taught English four hours a day and had sex for the remaining twenty. We travelled to France, drinking wine on the beach and failing to smoke cigarettes, nineteen years old, alone and the most good looking we would ever be in our lives.

One night we took the train to Monaco, won several hundred Euros playing roulette and spent it all on champagne. We said "I love you" to each other when we got back to Canada because we had both been intimidated by the raw, unfiltered romance of the European setting. I turned twenty, then twenty-one.

....

An authentic Mexican burrito is actually a rather plain mix of beans, meat, and rice or cheese. Chipotle has lied to us all. The over-stuffed, multi-ingredient, aluminum-foil-covered heavy diapers you think of as a burrito are known as Mission Burritos and originated in San Francisco in the 1960s. It is predicted that by 2018, Chipotle's annual sales will be more than $6.5 billion in the US alone.

....

Throughout my entire two-and-a-half years with Paul, I did not eat a single burrito. Not one. I knew they existed, of course. There was a Mexican restaurant in our little university town— Tacos El Asador. Our house was across the street and still I did not go there. (Poutine was really the It Food for students at the time. Now it is something called "poonair," a combination of poutine and donair that sounds like a great idea if you are eighteen and drunk and don't know how bad it's going to be to have a body later.) I ate all of the individual ingredients required for a complete burrito often, separately. I knew my way around a plate of homemade nachos better than most. I had experienced the odd taco night and was an accomplished fajita chef. I had a real boner for sour cream.

....

The frozen burrito was invented in 1964 in California and was an instant hit with grosso's everywhere. "Breakfast burritos" were invented some time in the early 1970s, for the same grosso's and their children.

....

A year older than me, Paul got into an overseas grad-school program midway through my third year. I sat with him in the campus newspaper office while he did his entrance interview. They liked him, I could tell. "Well," I offered, when he got off the phone. "We could break up. England is very far away. We could get back together when I come over next year." He would not hear of it. "What's the point?" he said. "We're going to be together a long time, next year included."

....

In October 1977, the face of Jesus appeared in a flour tortilla in Lake Arthur, New Mexico. The thumb-sized Jehovah-shaped mark in the tortilla stopped the production of Maria Rubio's husband's breakfast burrito. Within two years, over 35,000 people had visited the holy relic, which came to be known as the "Miracle Tortilla." Mrs. Rubio quit her job and worked full time presiding over the "Shrine of the Holy Tortilla."

❧

In November of 1977, a competing Miracle Tortilla appeared in the skillet of a Phoenix woman named Ramona Barreras. This time it was not just the face of the saviour, but the letters KJC and B, which stood, according to Ms. Barreras, for "King Jesus Is Coming Back."

❊

Several years later, in March of 1983, Paula Rivera of Hidalgo Texas found the face of Jesus in yet another corn tortilla and attempted to start a third, competing shrine. Pilgrims were loyal to the original Miracle Tortilla, and Ms. Rivera's shrine did not last long.

Months pass and it is Paul's 22nd birthday. His plane leaves the next day. We are celebrating this milestone with his family, at a Mexican restaurant. Mentally, I am already about two weeks into the tragic but beautiful yearnings of long distance, sending and receiving gorgeous love letters, pining dramatically by windows and in cafes, beatifically alone.

We arrive a few minutes ahead of everyone else and settle into a booth, looking over the menu. "I think I'll get a burrito," I say. "I don't think we should stay together when I go to England," he replies.

Black bean burritos are also a good source of dietary fiber and phytochemicals.

I had a few seconds to think about Paul's pronouncement. Mostly I made a high-frequency noise audible only to dogs and heartbroken teenage girls. The noise morphed into a strangled but bright "HELLO!" as I held back tears and shrieked a greeting at his parents, grandmother, and little brother, who had arrived together, all at once. I made small talk about my fourth year courses with the parents, discussed the menu with the grandmother, and asked the brother about his *World of Warcraft* stats. Paul tried to hold my hand under the table. This gesture was absolutely not returned.

In 2006 Panera Bread attempted unsuccessfully to prevent the opening of a Qdoba Mexican Grill, citing a contract granting Panera exclusive sandwich rights in the mall where Qdoba hoped to build. Superior Court Judge Jeffrey Locke heard testimony from chefs, culinary historians, and a high-ranking agricultural official before ruling that a burrito is not, legally, a sandwich. The delineating factor was quantity: a sandwich is two slices of bread, a burrito a single tortilla.

While Paul's dad ordered a round of drinks for everyone, I went to the bathroom and cried, ugly and loudly, for a long time. Not too long, obviously—I had to get back upstairs for margaritas. I spent a few minutes wiping my face clean of smeared mascara and the shattered pieces of my girlish dreams for the future, and returned to the table.

Our food had already arrived. Paul was staring at me and I knew he knew I had been crying. He gave me an angsty look that said, "Sorry." I gave him a look that said, "Kill yourself." I slid into the booth beside him, stopping at enough of a distance that I saw his grandmother notice. "I've never had a burrito before," I said cheerily, trying not to blush or cry or stab Paul in the face with a fork.

....

The original Miracle Tortilla met its end in 2005, when Mrs. Rubio's granddaughter took it to school for show-and-tell. It was dropped by a careless student, and the thirty-year-old tortilla shattered instantly. The pieces now live in a special drawer in New Mexico, but I imagine they are not looked at often.

....

Obviously, my life was over. I was twenty-one and had been betrayed by my True Love. It did not matter that the food had arrived. I would never know true happiness and was destined to die alone, probably soon. I pictured my sad, single corpse, laid out with pitying family members around me, cold and—Holy Shit. Good Lord. I am sure I don't need to remind you what it feels like to taste a burrito for the first time.

Amazing, in short. Incredible. All my favourite sauces, fillings and flavours had been brought together and wrapped gently in the arms of my other favourite thing, warm bread. I could not believe I had never had one before. I ate quietly but with what I presume was visible purpose. For the first time, I experienced that thing where it's like, *should I keep eating this burrito? I'm pretty full and I probably can't but maybe I should just try? Just because the best stuff probably collected in the bottom and I won't eat all of it but... oh there it goes, looks like the whole thing is gone I guess?*

I did not need to deal with the Paul thing anymore. I needed extra cilantro. I was not bothered by heartbreak, but had a pressing and extreme interest in more green salsa. Sure, my chest cavity felt like someone had pooped in it (a phrase I actually used in one of our later terrible, melodramatic emails), but how bad could the world be, really, if this sheer amount of sour cream could exist as part of a single meal for one person? I was fine, he was fine, it would all be fine.

• •

I read a website today which assured me that "it is unlikely the Aztecs ever made anything approximating a burrito, but I bet they would have liked it if they had." I agree.

• •

When the plates were cleared, Paul's parents brought out a birthday cake. I abstained; I was too full. I sang "Happy Birthday" to him with his family and may even have smiled for a picture. I do not know where that picture is now, but I feel sorry for it.

Paul moved to England the next day, and a few months later I started seeing an old friend who became and stayed my boyfriend. During the first year we dated, the route between our two houses was home to six burrito restaurants. You know what they say: when God closes a door, he opens an artisanal Mexican-fusion food truck.

I Want To Talk To You
About Dips

꧁

You'll have to forgive the lack of a coherent introduction, but in talking about dips as with literally any dip, it's important to dive right in. It's three in the morning and I have just woken myself up with a real conviction that this women's guide to dips NEEDS to be written, so please give me a minute to collect my thoughts. You see, dips are a subject near and dear to my heart. If a collection of dips were a man, I would marry that man and become Mrs. Dips. As it stands, my current human, non-dip partner won me over by ordering pizza (a great start) and then sensually arranging a veritable buffet of dips and sauces on his kitchen table while we waited for the 'za to arrive. I know, I know, back up, ladies… unless dips become sentient, then someone will need to be there to pick up the pieces because I will be BUSY. Now, onto the important stuff:

Choosing Your Vessel

Foodie Fact: Most non-dip foods exist primarily as things to be dipped. In their *a priori* state they may be chips, vegetables, chips, pita, chips, edible bread bowls, or chips, but ultimately they are empty canvasses, crying out for a rich layer of spinach-y, mayonnaise-y paint. There is no hierarchy of textures here—soft, crunchy, gush-y (cherry tomatoes, you feel me?), whatever. Where no dipping options are available and no other humans are present, a quick swirl of a finger will do. All are welcome at the table of the dip.

Dip-to-Chip Ratio: The Golden Rule

You don't want to overwhelm the dipped object, but you do want to mostly overwhelm it. I like a full-coverage dip, with the thumb/forefinger pinch area as the only bit not experiencing some level of immersion. Cream- or mayonnaise-based dips are really the only place moderation is necessary, as it can be unpleasant to just spoon a large amount of, say, Pizza Pizza garlic dipping sauce directly into the mouth (for some people) (for amateurs). With fresher, veggie-based dips, more is more is mmmmmm.

A Note on Double Dipping

This is kind of a controversial topic, but mostly people need to chill out about the ol' DD. As a general rule, if you would hug everyone in the group you are with, double dip away. Work functions, public food (i.e. buffets, samples, etc.), and larger events where you don't know all attendees—these are not double-dip territory. For instance, you do not double dip at a work colleague's funeral. I repeat: do NOT double dip at a work colleague's funeral, no matter how good their Aunt Hester's feta-and-olive spread might be.

Haters to the Left

In a woman's life, there's a lot of shaming that happens: slut-shaming, fat-shaming, body-shaming, shame-shaming (when someone shames you for trying to shame them, sort of an I-am-paper-you-are-glue scenario but with shame). Another important—though often overlooked—one is dip-shaming. If you're going hard on some zesty bruschetta and a Nosy Neil wants to shriek, "WHOA, HEAVY DIPPING THERE, MAN," simply Dip Hard 2: A Good Day to Dip Hard, and then go about your business. Haters directly to the left. Surround yourself with good friends who understand what's important in life: trust, honesty, a sense of humour, and detailed knowledge as to when Costco puts its giant dip tubs on sale. You are welcome to join my friend group. We call ourselves "The Big Dippers." I want to get us jackets.

The Best Dips, In Order

In the lower ranks you have things like ranch (sorry, get out of here, what are you, American?), weird bad oily mistakes from the lower-quality pizza joints, and anything you've ever tried to whip together from low-fat stuff in your fridge. Dips are not a time for low-fat substitutes, unless that substitute is Greek yogurt, and even then. Moving up through the lesser salsas and French Onion offerings we come to the top-five dips of all time, starting in at number five with the oft-overlooked olive oil/vinegar combo, a true classic. The fourth-best dip in the world, scientifically, is tapenade. An odd choice, some may say, but some are goons, tapenade forever. Third-place honours fall on the humble-yet-fresh tzatziki. There is an eight-way tie for second place, which goes to: seven-layer bean dip, garlic aioli, sriracha, salsa-that's-been-in-the-fridge, Heluva Good Dip, Tesco's caramelized onion hummus, sweet chili sauce, and, of course, guacamole. First place is full-fat sour cream, end of discussion.

Dip freely, dip often, dip well. I believe in you.

The Yogurt Women

❋

Jamie Lee Curtis led us here.

The lifestyle experts and gracefully aging actresses did not tell us what would happen. "They wouldn't lie to us," we said. "I do feel like my bowel movements are both more regular and more rewarding," we said. "Now you are slaves to our overlord," they said. What we had thought at first was a simple focus group turned into a nightmare beyond our wildest imaginations. We are prisoners of probiotics, captives of Creamy Originals, bound by *bifidus regularis*. We are the yogurt women. History will not remember us.

Each day we rise for yoga at gunpoint. The area is not fenced in, but overlooks a beautiful cliff; one misstep and you are hurled off. Mothers, young women, the elderly—the cliff feels no mercy. We are careful with our Downward Dogs.

YOGURT: YOU'RE A WOMAN, AREN'T YOU?

By sunrise we have already eaten breakfast ("pouring yogurt") and begun our daily activities. We spend hours laughing in our assigned multicultural friendship pods. Our mouths are cracked and dry. When we first arrived, we had nothing to laugh about. Now, that does not matter. The absurdity of it all is enough to have us cackling like witches over never-ending cups of peppermint tea. Also, they put drugs in the tea.

The afternoon is the hardest. Machines push and pull our faces into ever-more wistful expressions, while thin-lipped instructors drill us on euphemisms for "laxative," "constipated," and "distinctly lacking in flavour and texture." On level four we squeeze into athletic pants, sports bras, and hoodies before marching laps around a shopping complex designed to work us into a yogurt-hungry sweat. It is uphill the entire time. Our feet ache from unwieldy high heels, our faces from smiling. Most horrifying of all, each week a new sacrificial Doubting Friend is chosen. We must all watch as one of our own is forced to say, "But it couldn't possibly be that good… it's just yogurt." She is force-fed three gallons of Yoplait and then eaten by wolves.

At dinner we try the new flavour ranges. It is dangerous work. We lost three girls in trials for the Intensely Creamy line. What hit the stores was less than 400% of the product's original intensity. One woman who survived three rounds of "Seriously Citrus" testing is puckered for life.

We have learned to fear January—non-dairy yogurt substitutes for those on new vegan diets. Anyone unlucky enough to be selected for this high-risk test group comes back changed. The words "Mocha Soy Dream" are enough to have us all scrambling for other duties: leading belly-dancing hour or group-sass, or teaching new inmates to "mmmm" effectively.

This week has been okay: low-fat Greek. Plain, simple. We do not speak of the sample period for "alternative fruit flavours;" we have seen things involving rhubarb that would make a grown man weep.

There is no delicate way to say this: we shit constantly. A diet comprised almost exclusively of lactic acid, various yeasts and bacilli, and artificial colouring will do that to a person. The supervisors love this; this means it is working. "One in three women reported easier, more frequent bowel movements," the magazine copy will read. What it will not say is that the other two died of dehydration.

And so, day after day, week after week, meticulously charted menstrual cycle after menstrual cycle, we fester. Ferment, really, like the innumerable vats of milk products in the coolers. In a way, we are ourselves *becoming* yogurt, and this whole messed up world is one big lonely woman's fridge. Still, there are some comforts to this life: although we have been taken from our loved ones, mistreated, and used as digestive crash test dummies for a large dairy conglomerate, none of us has ever had a yeast infection.

A Poem About Cheese*

❦

Shall I compare Brie to a summer's day?
Chèvre art more lovely and more temperate:
Gruyère doth shake the dear tastebuds of May,
And Cheddar's lease hath all too short a date;
Sometime too hot the eye of Parmigiano shines,
And oft is Swiss' gold complexion dimm'd;
And every curd from curd sometimes declines,
By chance or nature's changing course unserv'd:
But thy eternal odour will not fade,
Nor lose possession of that taste thou owest;
Nor milk shall brag thou wanderest in his shade,
When in eternal lines to time thou growest (blue)
So long as men can eat, or eyes can see,
So long lives this, and this gives life to cheese.

*This was submitted to a professor of English at Queen's University in
2009 as part of an essay on Edward Young's theory of imitation versus
imagination. From the professor's notes: "I like the flow of your sentences,
and your general style… the only issues for me were the moments where you
claim (not apparently tongue in cheek) that your poems are the equal of
Shakespeare's."

Eating In Bed:
We CAN Have It All!

❧

You're a strong, smart, independent woman. You work hard, you play hard, and this weekend you want to spend your precious leisure time as God HERSELF intended: eating spicy foods in bed. Obviously, "Should I eat in my bed or not" is as rhetorical a question as, "Should I starve to death in the comfiest place on earth," or "Should I just let Netflix keep on rolling now that it's already queued up the next eppy to play in three seconds." There are lots of reasons that a mature, capable young woman like yourself might want to eat in bed: sadness, sleepiness, laziness, a rude hangover, a very good new season of a TV show, bad weather, something someone said to you at the office that was way over the line, annoying roommates, mom burns... the list goes on. The real issue is not IF you should eat in bed, but HOW, and the answer is: carefully, and with the below tips in mind.

Because it's the freakin' weekend (™ Robert Sylvester Kelly, alleged sex offender) and you deserve this, the following guide is for you. Here's exactly how to eat in bed.

Linens'n'Things

Get your nice sheets on (clean ones, we are grownups here), and your good pajamas. Maybe a cozy old T-shirt and some sweatpants? The ones that your ex-thing left there that time and, come to think of it, if he left his pants what did he even go home wearing? I'm just brainstorming. Put on whatever feels comfiest and arrange your pillows just so. My personal fave move is the bed-couch, where you arrange a few pillows behind you and then two on either side like fluffy armrests. Get creative with your space; you're in it for the long haul. Remember pillow forts? Now's the time to innovate with a pillow-based bar and grill. If you're eating something dripping with sauce, 1) you are doing this exactly right and 2) maybe lay down a towel to catch any errant drips and save yourself sleeping in a stained bed. (We both know you're not doing that laundry.)

Use a Plate, You Filthy Animal

Crumbs—one of bed food's few unpleasant side effects—can be easily avoided by being a damn adult and using dishes. Dishes, in order of bed friendliness, are as follows: a giant Central Perk-style mug used as a bowl, an actual bowl, just the full pot you cooked the thing in, a box of cereal, a plate. Mostly you are looking to avoid crouton remnants or other hard, crust-based crumbs. The last thing you want to do is exfoliate your feet when you tuck them under the covers. Gross.

HomeScents

It's important to choose foods that are bed-friendly, in particular those that can sit at the side of your bed for a while without stinking up the room. A full jar of hummus is a no-no, for instance, because you are probably not going to eat a full jar of hummus in one go (unless you are my roommate Adam, who literally eats it with his hands, from the jar) (Hi Adam, thanks for supporting my work!). More important, the rest of the container will sit on the floor or bedside table stinking away until you have to break the rules and leave the bed to put it back in the fridge/crack a window. Consider instead a giant bowl of pasta with olive oil and garlic (a "Why Doesn't He Love Me Anymore" classic), breakfast cake ("getting fired means not going into work on a Monday, ha, ha"), or my favourite meal: any kind of cheese on any kind of bread.

Sheets Happen, Not Sh*ts

No info or tips here, just 500-thread count, Egyptian-cotton, hotel-quality puns. If there was a tip to be gleaned from this honestly fairly thin joke, it would be: leave your bed to go to the bathroom, don't pee or poo in your bed. Good tip! And an important sentence to preserve forever in print!

Make the Most of Your (Lying) Down Time

Watch a bunch of movies. In a row, if you want. Write some letters to old buddies or crack one of the pseudo-intellectual magazines you keep in a mounting pile next to your bed, just in case. I know all the sleep experts tell us to use the bedroom only for sleeping, but I feel like those people have never experienced the rush of tending to one's work correspondence while snuggled under a duvet. The sheer thrill of being so productive while wearing a onesie in a semi-reclined state is unlike anything else. In short, pick a hobby and do it in your bed while snacking to maximize your relax. Relaximize.

People will tell you you're being gross. People are haters. A Bed Buffet is God's greatest gift. Prepare your giant bowl of Froot Loops and put on the sweatpants you got for free at that thing and make like former French president, Nicolas So-cozy. Or controversial daytime television host, Cozy O'Donnell. Or important philosophical text, Plato's Symp-cozy-um. Bon Appetit.

Pizzas I Have Loved

※

If there's one thing I know, it's that love changes you. I know five or six other things, but this is the thing I know most certainly. True love—the kind that grabs you at first bite—doesn't ever really let go.

I met Roger when I was seven, at a school-wide pizza lunch. He was $2 and came with a ginger ale, and the whole thing felt special from the start. I had ordered plain cheese on the little print-out form they'd given us a month earlier, but when he arrived just smothered in pepperoni, I didn't object. I accepted him for who he was: a greasy, pepped out corner piece. (A *corner piece*.) That day with Roger was magic. Pure, innocent—these were the days before dipping sauce. But I had no idea what was to come.

I LOVE YOU MORE THAN PIZZA.

JUST KIDDING. LUV U, PIZZA.

Next came Donnie. During an administration-sanctioned lunch off school grounds I went to my first panzerotto parlour. Naive and inexperienced, I immediately ordered a cheesy slice—getting a little wild, I thought, by including vegetable toppings. "We only do panzerottos," the heavyset Greek man behind the counter drawled. "Is that like pizza?" I asked. (Oh, to be young again!) "Sure."

Reader, I was not ready.

Donnie was plunked down onto my plate without any explanation; I was awestruck. He was... huge. Heavy. Girthy. A steaming bundle bursting at the seams—the equivalent of three slices, at least—and all for me. Donnie was my teenage Everest. I bit in. An instant mess. Steam and sauce and cheese and rather more mushrooms than I had anticipated oozed onto the plate, the floor, my pants. I slogged through, nervous and excited, full by the halfway point but determined to finish. My mouth and my body were tired; it was hard to tell who was more stuffed, me or Donnie. It was, to quote the elderly Rose DeWitt Bukater, "The most erotic moment of my life." I went back to class red-faced and panting, with grease on my corduroys. It was my first lesson in sensual gluttony, but not my last. Whenever I'm bloated and tired simultaneously, I think of Donnie.

In high school I did not see a lot of pizza. It was too busy with the popular girls. One summer I went to Italy, but what happened between myself, Roberto, Marco, Giovanni, Luka, Matteo, two different Albertos, Giuseppi, and Bianca is not fit for print. I will treasure the memories always, and pray those pictures never reach the Internet. Sometimes at night the wind whispers *Margherita*...

My university days saw a devolution—we all make mistakes—and an obsession with bad pizzas, the kinds that treated me rough, and left me reeling. They never looked like they did on the box. Once, in a drunken stupor of mayoral levels, I went to take Mikey—one of many shitty frozen pizzas I was involved with—out of the oven and the tray slipped from my hands, cheese and sauce making its way down the back of the hot grill. There it stayed overnight, baking on and forming a hard layer of toppings, turning my oven wall into a pizza with a metal crust. The next day I chipped Mikey off and ate a bit. What did I care? It wasn't what I wanted, but at least the crust was stuffed.

The cycle was intoxicating: the cravings, the cheap rush, the empty calories, the deals. The Coke-fuelled binges and the next-day dairy and gluten hangovers. The 2 AM screaming fights ("You're NOT delivery, you asshole, and you never will be!"), and gentle make up feasts at 3 AM, once the timer finally, inevitably, went off. It was messy, but it was honest. Hunger, pure and simple. The body wants what it wants, when it wants it. I called and Mikey—or someone like him—answered. Simple as that.

Eventually I'd had enough of waking up in an empty bed full of crumbs, of cleaning up greasy styrofoam the morning after. Slowly, I started to extricate myself from the cycle of shame. I made friends with some really cool vegetables. I even started seeing a carrot for a while. Jerry was good to me, but I won't pretend he wasn't a bit bland. Maybe that's what got me hitting the sauce.

I don't know who came up with the idea of adding a mayo-based dip to an already deeply rich and fat-heavy meal, but they are NAU-GHTY. I hit that creamy garlic lifestyle *hard* and I never looked back. See you later, Jerry. I drenched Paul,

Michael, Adnan, Loretta, Bob and countless others in sauce until they were unidentifiable. I took my fetish online, seeking out coupons for extra dipping sauces, ordering two even though the pizza was for one. I found myself on a site listing hacks for "custom sauces," creamy garlic mixed with dill, barbecue mixed with ketchup, just a tub full of mayonnaise on its own. Things got worse and worse. I'd wake up with no recollection of the night's proceedings, my mouth reeking of Zesty Marinara. Once, I licked a glob I found in the kitchen that turned out to be a heavy-duty rust removal gel. I was a fiend for the D. It wasn't healthy.

It got even worse when I moved to England, where I started what was probably my saddest relationship yet. Papa John always delivered, but he made me pay for it. Boy, did he. Familiar but vaguely exotic, he offered me extra cheese and something called a "Mexican Chicken Fiesta." He was there for me during those long nights indoors, and calmed me when the weather was bad, which was always. He wasn't exactly what I wanted, but who was? I spent many a night succumbing to pizza comas he had administered with care and jalapeño poppers. One particularly dark evening, feeling bored and a little reckless, I called him up and ordered "All The Meats." Oh, Papa. It was, as a housemate described, "Kind of too many meats?" But by then I didn't care. I tore at the soft dough, plunged my teeth into the gritty meat, licked up extra sauce as it dripped down my chin. It was empty calories but I was empty, too. He was total garbage and I loved it.

The night of All The Meats would be a turning point for me, though I didn't know it then. As the cheese burns healed and the sun came up, I came downstairs to discover that the leftover jalapeño poppers had solidified, and the remaining meats had congealed in an anonymous pile. And that's when I realized: John didn't love me. He never would. None of these crusty old pizzas were Roger, and they never would be. That little square from '95 was gone forever. As the sun rose over the Thames, I mourned my innocence, wished life could be more, and ate the remaining poppers and meats.

These days, things are calmer. A few years ago I joined an organic farming commune where I met a really nice quinoa salad. Stephen is kind, stable, and a complete protein. We have a great time together and it's very loving. Once in a while we invite the avocado smoothie next door to join us for a little fun. We all have very clear boundaries with each other, and there's a lot of respect between us. It's good, clean fun. Waking up with Stephen every day is a gift. Do I miss the old days of empty carbs and sauce-fuelled binges? Only every day.

Only every goddamn day.

Should You Eat That

A Quiz

Let's start with what's important: what is it?

a. Some kind of food. At this point it could be anything. I hunger.

b. A bag of candies!

c. A home-baked treat/wholesome lunch/rustic salad/Whole Foods original product.

d. My partner's oiled body.

How hungry are you, on a scale from 1 to 10?

a. A thousand. If I saw a living man right now I'd rip him to shreds and feast on his corpse.

b. Like a 5 or 6.

c. I hover constantly around a 4 or so, but I'd say I'm rounding the corner on 5 at the mo. The aromas! The BOUQUET!

d. 69 ;)

How do you feel about the food you're holding?

a. Anytime I look away from this precious morsel, all I see are cartoonish versions of the food dancing before my eyes, taunting me.

b. I'm not proud of what I did to get it, but I'm glad it's here. So glad. Finally, a moment for me.

c. Oh boy, this is a real treat. It's not every day I get to eat something so organic/foraged/deconstructed/kale.

d. It might be more accurate to say *it's* holding *me*.

Will eating this thing make you feel bad about yourself?

a. I can't imagine feeling anything worse than my stomach at this moment. Yesterday, I made friends with a doll I made out of tree bark. Then I ate the doll.

b. The cries of grubby children are something I got used to long ago. I can handle this. I deserve this. And I need the sugar rush to get me through the day.

c. I mean, it's carbon-neutral *and* artisanal. It's hard to picture something I'd feel better about!

d. We're all just castaways on the sexy seas of life, my friends. Nothing to do but float.

Who's around you right now?

a. Now that Twigsy's gone, I'm alone with my hunger. Forgive me, Twigsy.

b. A bunch of jam-hands children screaming for "their" candy.

c. Just some baristas, and they're not people, right?

d. Friends, play-partners and other tantric adventurers.

THE SANDWICH SPREAD MILLENNIALS ARE CALLING "FINE"

NOW WITH 100% MORE URBAN ENNUI!

"Are you sure you want to eat that?"—your coworker
a. Go fuck yourself, Carol.
b. Seriously?
c. What's your problem, Carol? Why are you like this?
d. Go fuck yourself, Carol... but wait up.

Mostly A's
You've been stranded on a deserted island for months without food, of course: EAT IT.

Mostly B's
You have literally stolen candy from a baby. Take a moment to consider this a true Life Low, but of course: EAT IT.

Mostly C's
You are the kind of person who would call themselves "a foodie." You're a terrible person, but of course: EAT IT.

Mostly D's
You have confused sex for food. Join the club. Now EAT IT.

On Splitting The Bill And
Other Nightmares

❋

1. Everyone is late. The restaurant, Apiculture, popped up mere hours before you got there, so there appears to be no waiting area. You don't know which of your friends made the reservation, so you wait outside in the cold, staring at the table for six through a hexagonal window.

2. Twenty minutes later you watch through the same window as your friends are seated, drinks in hand. "The vestibule is in the back," Tomas explains. "They kind of play by their own rules here."

3. Tomas picked the place. He knows all the best restaurants. "They make everything in-house," he says when you ask about the buzzing from the floorboards. "We're technically inside a beehive right now!" When Michael nervously protests—allergies—Tomas shoves a honey-glazed rib in his mouth. "Relax, guys. This place is amazing. Get into the locavore spirit!"

4. "Can I start you off with some cocktails?" the waitress asks. All the workers are female, you note. Sexists. She's not even wearing a skirt, just a shirt and socks and shoes. The pad of paper she's carrying is impossibly small, like her baby-sized polo shirt and her tiny ankle socks. It's like she was zapped with a shrinking ray that only affected her accessories. She has tired eyes.

5. The cocktail list does not include the cost of drinks. In fact, the whole menu is devoid of prices. Each entree has the words, "You'll pay at the end," scrawled beside it. This makes you nervous but everyone else is already drinking, so you push forward and order a "South American Stinger," a mix of bourbon, honey, nectar-infused bitters, and soft grains.

6. Tomas is so excited. He has Instagrammed the washrooms, the table, his feet—if the cocktails don't come soon his tweeting will take a dark turn. You hope he doesn't make a scene like the ones at brunch over the last six weekends. The rest of you are hungry and the constant, low buzzing is very disorienting but hey, it's Tom's birthday and you love him, this is his night.

7. A sign on the wall reads: "CASH ONLY | NO SUBSTITUTIONS | RESPECT THE QUEEN." "Oh, great," you think. "I wonder if they have an ATM."

8. The cocktails arrive. Yours is delivered inside a closed flower, and is impossible to drink without a proboscis. "I live for the Caesars here," says Tomas, taking a full, cooked lobster off a stir-stick. He negotiates around a burger, two fruit kebabs, and a party-size shrimp ring to reveal a mason jar of red liquid stuffed with celery and carrots. "So cute."

9. Tomas has brought novelty hats. He makes everyone wear one. Yours breaks.

10. You've been at the restaurant for two hours already and Tomas has drunk six Caesars, despite everyone else conspicuously stopping after round two. The table is littered with rimming salt and lobster shells. Michael and Sara are drunk, Alana looks sad and Steve is texting. You've nursed your Stinger so long it's mostly ice. The waitress is putting delicious looking food on everyone else's tables— cheese matured in beeswax, propolis smoothies, toast with royal jelly, something called "pupaella." The smells are intoxicating.

11. When the waitress comes back you plan to order a side salad and tell her "tap water's fine, thanks." She will look at you with the quietly judgemental air of a person relying on tips to pay her rent. She will look at you and a "10% at best" sign will illuminate itself in neon above your pathetic, student loan-ravaged head. You don't belong here and you both know it. It's just like Tomas to pick a place so clearly out of your price range.

12. "You know what would be fun? If we just ordered a bunch of things for the table to share. Like tapas!"

13. The food keeps coming and you all keep eating, like pigs at a trough made from found east-coast driftwood. You had hoped there would be free bread to fill up on, but it's mostly flowers and leaves and sap. The restaurant "doesn't offer" tap water, so you agree to bottled and think about what excuse you'll use to opt out of dessert. You calculate how much money was in your bank account this morning and wonder if rent has come out yet. You see Sara across the

table doing the same thing. When you lock eyes you both say, "This place is so great," very loudly. Tomas doesn't even hear; he's brainstorming hashtags.

14. It's decided: #T4dinz. "Tomas Turns Twenty-Two, plus dinz, duh." Below, the bees hum softly but insistently, continuing their delicate dance.

15. Four courses have come around. Your hands are sticky; you feel slightly drowsy. Michael's blotto. He's looking at you like he's got five eyes. His face touches the table and briefly fuses to it—everything's coated in honey and residue from pollen. You're all bloated, bursting, defenceless. Tomas claps his hands maniacally, and makes a complicated hand signal at the waitress, presumably looking for more drinks.

16. The realization that this place will probably not offer separate bills hits you at the same time as the waitress's pheromone-soaked rag.

17. You come-to in an unfamiliar, high-ceilinged room. The buzzing is louder now; it forms a sonic fog that fills the cavern. You wonder when the desserts are coming, if they'll remember that you asked for yours without the honeycomb. You wonder how hard it would be to free yourself from these plant-based restraints. You hate this restaurant.

18. Michael is dead beside you on the ground, more boils than person. His medic alert bracelet digs into his pink, swollen flesh. Ugh, Michael. Always running out on the bill. Now you'll be splitting it between only four of you—three, probably, because it's Tomas' birthday. Your bee captors dance around you victoriously while you fumble with your iPhone's tip calculator. The waitress seemed really nice, so you want to get the amount right.

19. Sara and Alana look terrified, and so are you. Without anyone to stop him, Tomas is likely to order a round of coffees for the table even though you're trying not to drink caffeine these days and you can get tea so much cheaper at home. The queen is addressing her people in some kind of private bee language; she seems angry.

20. Tomas rounds the corner before the cocoon has completely enclosed you. "I'm so sorry, Tara, forgive me," he weeps. "Also, do you have any change? I've only got fifties. Or I could put it on my card and you guys could p—" Drones drag him away before you even get a chance to reject the idea. As you slip into the darkness, you leave a two-star review on Yelp. "Too many bees."

2

WHAT'S GOING ON
WITH YOUR BODY

Ways My Body Is Being
Sneaky Right Now

※

One day I woke up and my body was different. Not different, but… sneaky. I noted it with some alarm until this pattern of bodily behaviour became my new normal. For now, at least, I have a sneaky body. Hormonal changes skulk around in the night, bumping into rogue hairs doing that Pink Panther creeping move, elbows and knees bouncing up and down to comedy-sneaking music. My breath is shifty too, having quietly developed problems processing coffee that were not previously there. And my armpits, good Lord. They're in a secret sweat club with the backs of my knees (!), and I do not know when the meetings are but I would like to attend and object.

Look, I'm not ungrateful. Aging is a beautiful gift—in that it is the opposite of being dead—and life is a gift, that's WHY they call it the present, hello, read the embroidered pillows at Pottery Barn. I am deeply pleased not to be dead, almost every day, and thankful for the wisdom and depth that each passing year brings to my life (give me two seconds, I'm just buying some crocheted

ADULTHOOD IS 20% DOING
YOUR LAUNDRY REGULARY, &
80% COMING TO TERMS WITH
YOUR FACIAL MOLE.

cat-cozies on Etsy to go with this statement). But yikes, what is going ON with the way my butt fits jeans now? And a hundred other things. I guess it's time for a list:

I Somehow Got a Grown-Up's Face and No One Told Me

I had some nice pictures taken of myself the other day for work purposes or comedy stuff or whatever, and while they are perfectly fine photos and will certainly serve their purposes, they also did something unexpected and kind of rude: they tapped me on the shoulder and whispered in my ear, "You are not nineteen." I know this, of course. This has been true for years now, and, in the adapted words of Hannah Horvath's gynecologist, "You couldn't pay me to be [19] again."

However.

While I was vaguely aware that time was passing, I don't know if I realized that I was also aging. I just thought I was gaining life experience and a deeper appreciation for my friends and family and an awareness of the value of Investment Bras while maintaining the tight, bright skin of my teens and hi, no I'm not. I still get carded at the liquor store sometimes, but when I smile my face crinkles up and I have a new, real love for products that combat "dark circles." OH AND: I found my first real wrinkle. My first, "Hello, nice to see you, I am the spectre of your body's inevitable decay," wrinkle. It is a sarcasm crease above my right eyebrow from raising it like a snarky emoji. And I LOVE IT. Because that's the thing about your body and face, it shows how you've used it. Isn't that cool? As it turns out, I have used my face to be incredulous a lot. This jerk-wrinkle has made me excited about further wrinkles, and especially laugh lines; what a lovely idea laugh lines are. "Oh these? This is just a visible measure of how much happiness I've had in my life. On my face, every day." Fine with me.

I Don't Even Want to Get into the Hair Issue

Just kidding, I want to get into all the issues, all the time. Not "The Issues," obviously, because I am not the person to talk to about Syria or green infrastructure, much as I wish I was; but when it comes to the importance of Rogue Body Hair, I am your girl.

I'd like to start this off with a brief memo to moles—ATTN: MOLES, what is going on with your hair production, guys? Why is everything so wiry and dark and frighteningly rapid? How did a previously hairless mole recently sprout three supersonic pitch-black friends that need to be carefully tended to at all times because they apparently grow OVERNIGHT? Urgent memo, plz respond ASAP, I have a strapless dress I want to wear next week.

Hair Issue Pt II

Related: twenty-six seems to be the age of the long, lone chin hair. This has been confirmed by friends the world over, and once four or more women have texted you, "I know right?" about something, it is fact. A single, dinglin' chin hair just happens for us all around twenty-six years of age. Having passed this milestone just last June, I am now the proud owner of a solo hair on my upper neck that ripens like an avocado: not ready, not ready, BOOM, RIPE AND YOU MISSED IT, now you are out in public frantically fingering the delicate beginnings of a mini-beard. This thing will stubbornly remain too short to pull out for weeks, hanging out quietly and unobtrusively until all of a sudden I reach up and it's a visible, lengthy strand, and I am on the streetcar, desperately yanking at the world's sparsest long-white beard like a panicked, crap wizard.

Something is Going On with My Breasts

This is not an emergency of the chin-hair variety, although if we're perfectly frank there has been a lone nip-hair sighting (my boyfriend, thoughtfully, both pointed and plucked it out like the goddamn gentleman that he is). I feel like I still have some time, here. But I can also feel them doing... something. Shifting. Widening. They are heavy in a way that they were not before. I mentioned this to a friend in her thirties who said it was "only the beginning," and then suggested that her entire body was in a race to pool at her feet, like JELL-O in a bag, and then we both went quiet and decided it was probably time for a nice glass of wine.

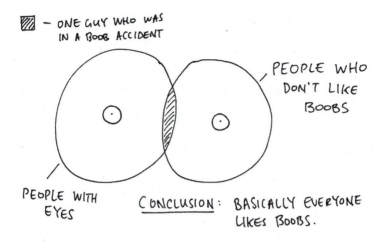

— ONE GUY WHO WAS IN A BOOB ACCIDENT

PEOPLE WHO DON'T LIKE BOOBS

PEOPLE WITH EYES

CONCLUSION: BASICALLY EVERYONE LIKES BOOBS.

Hair Issue Pt III: The Never-Ending Story

In addition to, "You need to pee after sex," "Your neck might just go weird and there's not much you can do about it," and, "No one can take pretty eyes away from you, cling to this forever," I wish someone had told me: "Your pubes do not stay shaped like a triangle in perpetuity, but rather creep outward towards your thighs over time like out-of-control ginger-y vines, and please when describing this phenomenon later in your life on a women's website do not make a red sea/high tide metaphor, it will only serve to gross everyone out." Consider these truths NOTED.

Anyway, we're all going to shit and I think it's kind of beautiful. If only we were allowed to do it in peace.

The Freelance Diet and Exercise Program

❋

Are you looking to get in shape? Trying to slim down or "fit up"? Have you recently decided to stop treating your body like a garbage can labelled "Pizza Only"? Well done, you disgusting slob! I'm excited for you. We at the Monica Heisey Centre for Freelance Fitness And Like A Good Diet Too I Guess are all excited for you.

But what's a day in the MHCFFLAGDT life like? What can you expect from the program, aside from RESULTS? Why *tell* you, when we can *show* you:

9 AM—11 AM: 2 hrs Sit Ups. By placing your alarm clock just out of reach and slightly above your bed, you'll be doing hundreds if not thousands of sit ups daily, simply to press snooze! The more crunches you want to do, the earlier you can set that alarm you know you'll never, ever pay attention to.

11:15 AM: Make a green juice (200 cal.)

11:16 AM: Instagram a green juice. Remember: it only takes two minutes to Google "what is spirulina," but you can tweet about consuming it for up to six hours! It's important to keep your personal brand in shape, too.

11:30 AM: Breakfast of Champions: bread. Just bread (200 cal.)

11:35 AM: 10 mins Walking, to coffee shop. Jogging can be substituted for walking if you're an advanced practitioner of the program or if you saw someone across the street you don't want to talk to. Drink one cup of whatever is hot (literally) and cool (figuratively).

12:30 PM: 5 mins Abdominal Crunches from laughing at own joke about what if the bat signal was for butts, i.e. a "butt signal."

12:45 PM: 10 mins Sweat Therapy. Read email from parents asking about stalled payments on loan from last year's taxes. Flip between personal banking tab and the email, slowly levelling up resistance to the idea of paying them back at all.

1:00—1:30 PM: Craft a "To Do" list. Include "love myself" as a task and check it off first.

2:00 PM: Begin actual day's work.

3:00 PM: 15 mins Web-Based Hypnotherapy. Get approximately five or six pages deep Googling celebrity lunch descriptions. Wonder if it's possible to ever get tired of grilled chicken breast and steamed vegetables. Wonder if you have either. Get hungry.

3:15 PM: Lunch of Champions: bread (400 cal.)

3:30 PM: 10 mins Stretching. Focusing on core groups such as hamstrings, quadriceps, and The Truth. Do some light yoga while on the phone to your parents, telling them you've been saving up for a mutual fund. Feel a warm calmness radiate through your body as they say, "Monica, please, $500 installments every two weeks, like we agreed. And your sister told me you bought shoes." Namaste.

3:45 PM: Google "mutual fund."

4:00 PM: 20 mins Cycling. Cycle through Facebook, Instagram, Pinterest, Tumblr, Twitter, Snapchat, and several Deep'n'Meaningfuls on Gchat before beginning actual day's work.

4:20 PM: lol

4:21 PM: 10 mins Walking. Leave house in search of any food that is not bread. Advanced practitioners can add a high-impact cardio workout by finding out that the cute barista with the tattoos knows your name.

4:31 PM: Return with a different kind of bread.

5:00 PM: Begin actual day's work.

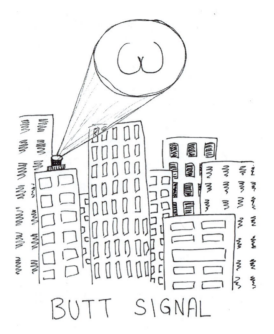

BUTT SIGNAL

6:15 PM: Survey what you've done: a short story called "Buttman Saves Gotham" and a listicle about different ways to enjoy scarf season.

7:00 PM: Antioxidant Therapy. Consume between 2 and 5 glasses of red wine (0 cal.) (There's no information on the bottle about this.)

8:30 PM: Romantic Interlude. The preferred fitness tracking app of the MHCFFLAGDT does not recognize sexual activity as exercise, to which we contend, "why's it got the word "active" in it, then." Instead input between 3 and 30 minutes of "general dancing" plus a few tricep exercises (from high fives).

8:45 PM: Dinner of Champions: toast (600 cal.)

9:00—10:00 PM: 1 hr Wait Training. Spend 60 minutes contemplating the multitude of cheques and direct deposits you have been promised for your work but so far have not seen. Check and re-check the spreadsheet you made that time. Wait.

11:00 PM: Light post-dinner snack. Consume whatever is left in the fridge, cupboards, and convenience store across the street (approx. 1500 cal.)

12:00 AM: Check blood pressure by Googling ex's name + "success."

12:30 AM: 1.5 hrs Light Therapy. Work on your secret shame novel in the dark, illuminated only by the healing glow of your laptop.

2:00 AM: Sleep well, fitness warrior. Tomorrow is another day.

Welcome To Your Mid-Twenties
Love Your Pal, Creams

❋

Hey girl!

It's me—your old pal, Expensive Creams. Or should I say your NEW pal! God, we're going to have so much fun together, you have no idea. It's going to be wild. I have been waiting and waiting and waiting for this day. You must have seen me, surely. On your mom's shelves? In the windows of fancy department stores, wrapped up like precious gems from exotic lands? Ohhhh, buddy. I've been watching since you were breaking into the medicine cabinet and slathering Pond's all over your face till you were pasty white and crumbling like some kind of moon child. What you didn't realize was that you were just practicing the extreme-y, creamy measures you would one day take in a futile attempt to stop the relentless pull of gravity. But you can't, of course, and now that bitch Gravity is working its natural forces on your sweet baby's face.

Look, I get it. As a woman there are many frightening things you face every day: institutionalized misogyny; rape culture;

meeting someone who definitely knows your name but you don't know theirs and they can tell; white pants; the "boho" trend… the list goes on. And then the list stops, because it reaches the No. 1 enemy of everyone, everywhere: WRINKLES.

That's right, babygirl, I see you. And I see those creases forming in your forehead and around the sides of your mouth and around your eyes when you smile. "But Creams," you might say. "Why don't you just back up off me and let me age how I want, there's nothing technically wrong with wrinkles and also, I'm twenty-six so I feel like you're getting a little ahead of yourself."

Listen up: I see how you treat that vintage purse of yours, all nasty and scuffed and faded. You think your face is going to get it any better? Not without me, it's not. You are the purse, and your face is hard-worn leather from the '80s. You need me. You need me like the 1960s needed the British power rock trio that shares my name. You need me like Pharrell Williams NEEDED to bring the world Qream, the milky liqueur we'd been waiting for. You need me like "peaches and… " Got it?

Don't tell me you haven't noticed the toll of your mid-twenties: the hangovers that last a hundred days, the inability to process dairy, the whatever is going on with your butt. You see it. I see it. It's happening, and it's real. And one day, one day soon, it will drive you into the sweet, sweet arms of Creams. We're used to a little resistance off the top. But eventually you'll remember those four magic words, passed down through your mother, your friends, in lifestyle magazines and targeted Facebook ads and out of the perfect mouth of Our Mother Beyoncé: *wash off your makeup.*

And at first maybe you are just washing off your makeup. But one day you'll walk by a Kiehl's and think, *I don't know what toner is but maybe I should get some.* And you will. You suuuuure will. A few weeks of nightly cleansing and bi-nightly toning and you'll start to wonder, *Should tiny micro-beads be exfoliating my face before bed?* They should. Once you're comfortable with the microbeads, a whole world will open up before you. Exfoliants

FOREVER JUNG

really are a gateway product. I give you two years before you're buying shit packed with crushed-up sea creatures and expensive pseudoscience. Welcome to the cosmoceutical rabbit hole, my precious. We've been waiting, photosensitive light-enhancing foam at the ready. Revitalizing microcules on deck. We've been aerating our oxyjuvenators and upping the shine on the shine-activation particles, because now is our time.

Soon you'll be ordering boutique essences off Korean websites to complete your twelve-step nightly routine, then eventually you'll find you're actually aware of what salicylic acid does. You'll wake up in the middle of the night to discover yourself mixing face masks in your kitchen with a mortar and pestle like some kind of modern-day sorceress. One day, one day soon, you'll know the difference between a collagen night mask and a collagen eye cream, why you prefer your anti-oxidants to come from pomegranate oils, and what brands of serum you prefer in the $60-$100 range.

And you know what? You're going to love it.

Stop frowning, honey. You'll get lines. Creamz OUT.

What To Wear To Barf
At 30,000 Feet

※

Of all the things about fashion I find perplexing (and there are many), nothing is more confusing to me than what people choose to wear to the airport.

Airport fashion in 2015 seems to fall into two camps. Either: "I consider the plane an extension of my bedroom, why isn't there Netflix on this aircraft," or: "I am not exactly sure what an airport is, but it sounds like it is probably some kind of club. I have thus come Ready2Dance and in shoes that will not be useful when I arrive in Regina, Saskatchewan."

Having spent a few years studying and then working overseas, I have some experience with airports, and feel like I have Airplane Attire down to a science. That science can really be boiled down to the following consideration: *how cozy-yet-fancy do you look?* The goal of airport dressing is to appear comfortable, physically and financially, like you could be Hilary Swank but no one can say for sure, because you're dressed very low key and seem so down-to-earth.

Look at rich people in the airport, the ones boarding ahead of you. The ones eating little bundles of complimentary nuts and sipping mimosas as you try to cram your overstuffed carry-on in the overhead bin next to someone's cat carrier. These people are almost certainly wearing the following: a cashmere sweater, some kind of dangly necklace, easy-to-remove boots, leggings that cost more than your rent, and a big old scarf. That's it! It's not complicated.

Basically, you need to dress so it looks like a mistake that you are in coach. A grievous mistake, which should be corrected quickly but tactfully by a helpful stewardess, who will reinstate you in your seat/bed and quiet you with complimentary champagne and a handful of the expensive kind of nuts. This has happened to me exactly once, but one go in the seat/bed with the fancy nuts and the free champagne was enough to inspire me to assemble a Designated Airplane Outfit, complete with stolen cashmere sweater (thanks Dad), regular leggings, easy pull-on boots, and a big ol' scarf. It was A Look, and I was (and am) committed to it.

Sadly, this is not a story of the time my easygoing-yet-upscale style led to a seat in first class and a set of free pajamas gently gifted to me at 30,000 feet. This is, in actuality, a story about barf.

Psyched you out with the intro there, but I'm sorry to tell you, this is a spew narrative. It is a cautionary tale, an important reminder that even the most meticulously-planned plane attire cannot save us from fate, a modern fable about the time my cashmere-swaddled hubris came back to bite me in the jeggings-covered ass. But mostly, it is just a hard-and-fast story about barf.

I mean it, guys. If you're not into a long and detailed narrative of spew, turn back now. This is a tale of vom, a ton of vom, and nothing but the vom, so help me Vom. Strap in if you're ready for it, yak-aficionados.

On this particular day, a day that will live in Vom-famy, I boarded my flight to England with the mixed emotions particular to leaving a place one has always considered "home," to return to the new place rapidly becoming it. Exacerbated by a rushed but lovely dinner with my mom, and my dad's hilarious and adorable but also really-kind-of-emotional-if-you-think-about-it habit of refusing to leave the airport until I'm all the way through security and he can physically no longer see me, I felt a little queasy but presumed it was just nerves. I boarded the plane, ate the cruddy little Bolognese pasta and dry, sad chocolate cake provided to us plebs and went to sleep.

Then I awoke. The teen beside me was snoozing away with his hoodie over his face, but it was almost immediately clear to me that I needed to get out of my seat and into the bathroom for barf reasons. I nudged him awake. He looked at me the way I imagine he looks at his mom when she tells him to turn down the Dashboard Confessional. I awkwardly jangled all the seats in my immediate vicinity until I was in the aisle, then the bathroom.

I will spare you much of the graphic details of what followed, but I will add as a quick disclaimer that if you're going to attempt a barf-while-peeing maneuver in an airplane bathroom, do NOT try to wash that barf out of the sink by turning on the taps. You will make a watery barf stew that will threaten to slosh over the sides of the sink/all over your jeggings and underwear during the inevitable turbulence that will follow. This is how I lost the first part of my Designated Airplane Outfit. It is a testament to the unpleasantness-still-to-come that "carefully wrapping and throwing out my Bolognese-riddled underwear in the airplane bathroom" was not the apex of my day's unpleasantness.

The remaining hours of the flight were divided between weirdly sweaty naps and waking up the much-beleaguered teen (Sorry, dude. Who could have known?) to go to the bathroom and watch each part of my plane meal resurface into the sink.

Real Life Low, right? Surely the torture ended there, in my feverish plane nightmare world. No way it could get any worse at all, for indeed what could be worse than a bout of nausea spanning an entire transatlantic flight?

Well.

We hit some very bad turbulence during landing. Like, insanely bad. It was a real roller coaster ride of emotions, if all the emotions on the roller coaster were softly whispering "barf right now wherever you can." Wherever I could looked like it was going to be in my own pathetic little hand, so I grabbed my air sickness bag. I started to feel a bit better and the turbulence settled down. Just in case, I reached my aforementioned pathetic little hand inside the aforementioned air sickness bag to open it up, so that if I felt sick later I would have a receptacle.

And that is when I touched a stranger's cold barf.

As you may have guessed, this caused me to just chunder EVERYWHERE, everywhere mainly being all over my Designated Airplane Sweater (RIP DAS, you deserved so much more). I wrapped the barf-y sweater into itself like a nightmare panzerotto, tucked it under the seat in front of me with a quiet knitwear eulogy, and softly cried to myself while we landed. The teen was unimpressed. When we disembarked I took his air sickness bag with me, as it was becoming increasingly apparent that something was horribly wrong with my body and I should steel myself for more bad behaviour on the part of my internal organs.

In line at customs is when I reached what might be my most miserable point ever in life. Alone and surrounded by other tired and worn out (though less smelly/dishevelled) travellers, I felt more barf about to happen. Gross Barf Lady was my new identity, I had reached a kind of Stockholm Syndrome with my own body. This was my life now, I was the rightful mayor of Barf Harbour, Maine, the president of Vomania, the reigning queen of Spewtopia. I calmly reached for my air sickness bag and went to open it, and my mouth, at once, ready to get it all over with.

It was in this moment of calm acceptance that I realized the teen had put his gum in the bag, right at the top, sealing it shut.

My mouth filled with vomit as I clawed desperately at the cherry-scented wad of resin and spittle. Barf dribbled out of the corners of my mouth. Someone tapped me on the shoulder, and when I turned towards them to explain that this was NOT A GOOD TIME, I vomited all over a concerned customs official's shoes and pants. (As another hot tip, if you would like to expedite your passage through UK customs, a very efficient method is covering someone who works there in plane food and stomach bile.)

And so I walked out into the British morning (like the regular morning, but more polite) wearing only leggings and a tank top. Stripped of my travel armour I waited in line for a cab and sat in the back, writhing around in my own sweat, half sleeping and occasionally waking to barf. I noted glumly that it was a spectacularly crisp and beautiful morning, and the

Thames and all the usual landmarks looked unbelievable and I laughed and laughed because London really is a living fairytale land sometimes. But mainly, I thought about barf. I went home and the Chunder Express choo-choo-ed up the stairs and into my bathroom and there it remained for several hours. It was maybe the worst, and definitely the grossest, day of my whole life. And you know what, though? Pretty nice life.

After a few days of this I emerged from my room, pallid and ten pounds lighter and with a very disgusting anecdote for the right kind of dinner party. Eventually I acquired a new sweater to replace the old one (thanks Dad), and my Designated Airplane Outfit has an important, if déclassé, new addition: a large and varied collection of plastic bags.

Ice-Boner™

❀

On Sat, Feb 9, 2013 at 10:40 PM,
Michael Dwindly <mdogg@gmail.com> wrote:

Hi Angela,
I wanted to send you an email to clear the air, as it were.
It's been a rough couple of weeks for us both and I know
you're really going through something right now, but this
has got to stop. I also know you are still outside my house,
so I will see when you read this and request that you do
as I say and leave my neighbourhood upon receipt of this
email. I do not wish to involve the police in this matter
but feel my personal safety is at risk.

If you could also destroy the life-sized sex doll you made
out of my clothing and have been camping with, I would
greatly appreciate it.

Thanks and all the best in the future,
Mike

On Sat, Feb 9, 2013 at 10:41 PM,
Angela Sandsworthy <angel_a@hotmail.com> wrote:

YOU KNOW I CAN'T DO THAT MIKE. THIS IS
BIGGER THAN BOTH OF US.

On Sat, Feb 9, 2013 at 10:55 PM,
Michael Dwindly <mdogg@gmail.com> wrote:

Angela, please. I would never have signed up for that
after-work soccer team if I had thought this is how it
would end, but here we are. I am begging you once again
to CEASE AND DESIST, or I will be forced to take legal
action.

On Sat, Feb 9, 2013 at 11:03 PM,
Michael Dwindly <mdogg@gmail.com> wrote:

Where did you get a mini trampoline and what have you
done with your shirt?

On Sat, Feb 9, 2013 at 11:04 PM,
Angela Sandsworthy angel_a@hotmail.com wrote:

I'M COVERED IN OIL AND I WANT YOU, MIKE. I
WANT YOU SO MANY WAYS.

On Sat, Feb 9, 2013 at 11:11 PM,
Michael Dwindly <mdogg@gmail.com> wrote:

You were our firm's top administrator. You have not
reported in to work for weeks. You were on the road to a
promotion. This is beneath you.

On Sat, Feb 9, 2013 at 11:12 PM,
Angela Sandsworthy angel_a@hotmail.com wrote:

I STILL SEE IT AT NIGHT, MIKE. YOU. ME.
THE CO-ED LOCKER ROOM. THE DELICATE
MIST COATING YOUR BODY. THE SCENT, IN
THE AIR, OF AXE ICE-BONER™. I MUST HAVE
YOU, WHATEVER THE COST. I SMELL YOU IN
MY DREAMS. IF YOU WISH TO FUCK FURTHER
ABOUT THIS MATTER, COME ;) SEE ME
OUTSIDE.

On Sat, Feb 9, 2013 at 11:20 PM,
Michael Dwindly <mdogg@gmail.com> wrote:

You're better than this, Angela.

*>>>>angel_a@hotmail.com attempted to start a file
transfer: boobs.gif*
>>file transfer of boobs.gif not accepted.

On Sat, Feb 9, 2013 at 11:35 PM,
Michael Dwindly <mdogg@gmail.com> wrote:

It's time to go now, really. I can't be held accountable for the results of my cologne; I mean how was I to know this would happen? I'm just a simple guy who wants to smell like he's recently had sex with a glacier and will not be calling in the morning. Don't make this harder than it needs to be.

On Sat, Feb 9, 2013 at 11:36 PM,
Angela <angel_a@hotmail.com> wrote:

I'LL MAKE YOU HARDER THAN YOU NEED TO BE. VERY HARD INDEED. SEX-HARD.

On Sat, Feb 9, 2013 at 11:38 PM,
Michael Dwindly <mdogg@gmail.com> wrote:

You are a 47-year-old woman with a family. I have called Unilever to register a complaint, but their Ravenous Female Hoard Dispersal service is overloaded as a result of their recent WizardShaft spray. A representative from the company did come over to high five me, though, so I feel that they've done their due diligence. This is between you and me now. Let's leave the Ice-Boner™ out of it.

On Sat, Feb 9, 2013 at 11:40 PM,
Angela <angel_a@hotmail.com> wrote:

OH, ICE-BONER™. SWEET SENSUAL SCENT OF
THE GODS. I FELT LOVE BEFORE, I THOUGHT.
WITH THE RELEASE OF "WOODSY BALLS,"
"SLUT ELIXIR" and "THUNDERDICK" I CAME ;)
CLOSER AND CLOSER, BUT NONE OF THOSE
FRAGRANCES COULD HAVE PREPARED ME FOR
THIS. NOTHING HAS MADE MY BODY TINGLE,
MY SENSES SURGE, MY MENTAL FACULTIES
TOTALLY SHUT DOWN LIKE ICE-BONER™. MY
BRAIN HAS PUT ON A BIKINI. DO A BODY-SHOT
OFF MY HEART.

On Sat, Feb 9, 2013 at 12:00 AM,
Michael Dwindly <mdogg@gmail.com> wrote:

You sound like Kanye West. I'm calling the cops.

How I Kept Worrying And
Learned To Love Self-Care

✿

I am a fun person to have at parties because no one knows my secret. (Relax, this is not the part of the book where I reveal that I am a serial killer.) (That is in the Love and Sex chapter, duh.) I drink and eat and chatter like everyone else. I put on too much lipstick and talk too closely to the party's resident Attractives and stay well away from the playlist because I know that is not my purview. However, the one thing I am sure to hide from everyone is the moment of the party (and it is every party) when I look around the room, at the youth and the revelry and the cute outfits and tastefully quirky furnishings and think: "One day this will all be in the ground and no one will remember we were ever here."

FUN, right?

Some other chill, enjoyable activities I engage in are: thinking, just as I drift off to sleep, how similar a dreamless slumber probably is to the total oblivion of death, or wondering, when my boyfriend is fifteen minutes late coming home, if he's been struck by a car or pushed in front of a subway or simply slipped, these things happen, or imagining on planes how calm I would be if we just fell into the ocean and were never heard from again.

These are, of course, the most extreme examples. On an average day I probably only contemplate The Void like two or three times, with most of my hours occupied by lesser worries like, "Remember when someone said 'hi' and you said 'fine thanks, how are you'?" and "Is my mom right about hackers watching me through my laptop's webcam," and "If so, did they see me trying to do the 7/11 dance yesterday in my kitchen." I'm what is known colloquially as "a worrier," and what a therapist would probably call "an anxiety case." My particular therapist is very soft-spoken and polite and just says "you're you."

It took a long time to realize I was an anxious person, because for a while, my anxiety was a pretty helpful tool. I always had a route planned to get where the group was going, with an alternate route in case of traffic or accident or terrorist attack, whatever. I made plans preemptively, because I worried about people getting fed up with the planning portion of events and abandoning the idea of a hangout all together, leaving me alone and unloved. I fantasized about never getting anywhere in life, so I worked very very hard. Even the panic attack I had when faced with my Grade 10 math exam simply resulted in my mom swooping in to take me away from the offending arithmetic and me writing the test at a later date, in a quiet room supervised by my favourite teacher.

Of course, my anxiety was less helpful when I was waking my first boyfriend up at 3 AM, crying because I couldn't sleep and couldn't stop thinking about one day being dead, and would

I even get anything done before that happened? (Tip4Teens: if you are looking to slowly drive a 19-year-old boy away over time, try this!) It was less helpful when I spent the entire day after a party lying in bed wracked with shame, freaking out about saying something I felt I shouldn't have (Tip4Everyone: whatever you said was probably fine.) (Tip4Racists: not you). It became less and less helpful until I finally had to admit that it was a problem.

The terrible beauty of anxiety is that it can loop in on itself, becoming a catalyst for further angst. "I'm nervous about x," you think. "Ugh, it's so ridiculous that I'm nervous about that. Why am I such a stress case? I wonder if it's possible to worry so hard you give yourself cancer. Probably is, maybe I have it, I guess I'll spend the next three hours Googling 'worry cancer' instead of leaving the house. I'm a mess." It was in the middle of one of these spirals that I stumbled upon a forum for sufferers of chronic anxiety. People with names like WorriedMomOf3, ShyInLondon and Hopeless420 shared stories and tips and stress-management techniques. It was here that I was introduced to the concept of self-care, an idea that has helped quiet the "DEATH FAILURE TURMOIL ACCIDENTALLY FARTING IN FRONT OF MY CRUSH" side of my brain.

For the uninitiated, active self-care relies on the premise that we can and should make time in our lives to support and nurture ourselves. This means different things for different people but ultimately, it's about listening to yourself, understanding your own needs and fulfilling them. For me, self-care takes the form of healthy, home-cooked meals, saying "hell no" to events I don't want to go to, the occasional Powerful Woman's Bath (coconut oil, Epsom salts, lavender oil, red, red wine) and the non-judgemental cultivation of between four and seven To Do lists at any given time. It sounds simple, but initially it just felt like further fodder for my anxious inner voice: "you're taking too much time in the bathroom, that's selfish;" "three of these To Do lists are exactly the same tasks but in different orders;" "did you really need to include 'go outside' on your list just so you could cross it off;" "cookies are not a healthy home-cooked meal;" etc.

Women in particular are taught to give endlessly to others, to consider the needs of our friends and families and partners and coworkers before our own, to feel guilt about taking what we need, or—heaven forbid—want. It felt silly at first to get into a steamy bath and think, "Good for me." But it was good and is good. Good for me.

LIFE HACK:

TURN A NEGATIVE INTO A POSITIVE BY CHANNELING YOUR STRESS INTO A DECORATIVE RASH.

Self-care is not just for sufferers of anxiety or other mental health issues; there's literally nothing to lose by devoting time and energy to the task of taking care of yourself, no matter your mental state. Here then are some suggestions for developing your own self-care practice:

Think about What Really Makes You Feel Good

Hint: these are often the kinds of things we're told are "indulgences," but honestly, what is so indulgent about doing what you want to do?

Make a List of the Things You Like or Want To Do

Consider activities that will benefit your mental, physical, emotional, financial, and social well-being. Saving money can be self-care, but so can a DIY hair mask, a cheeseburger, or a night in watching movies with your best friend. Make a note of bigger things (a weekend in a cabin in the woods, a new dress that makes you feel like Kim Kar-freaking-dashian), and smaller, everyday moments of care (cleaning your bedroom, sitting still and enjoying where you are and what you're doing, a fancy latte). Keep the list handy so you can pull from it whenever you want to do something nice for yourself.

Carve Out Some Time to Actually Do These Things

The hardest part of self-care is finding time to devote to yourself. Modern life is busy and hectic and there is a lot of weird shame around being idle. Push past that feeling and book off a night to do whatever the hell you want, by yourself, for yourself. I can tell you right now that sometimes the best Saturday night you can have is one where you talk to no one and stay in your house knitting or reading or lighting various pleasant candles.

Have an Emergency Self-Care Plan

Had an especially awful day? Going through a break up. Just refreshing the page on your bank account over and over all day thinking about how you don't even know what a pension IS?

Instead of coming home from work and stress-drinking a bottle of wine, why not treat yourself to a nice massage or go out to a restaurant alone or spend a really long time painting little flowers on your nails? When I'm in an anxiety tailspin and I want to focus my brain on something else, I like colouring books. Very Zen, very calming, very "twenty-six going on twelve."

Never Feel Bad about It

As my wise friend Jocelyn once paraphrased from another wise person who probably read it in a book or something, "You have to put on your own oxygen mask before you can help those around you put on theirs." This is true on airplanes, and in life. Just like that other rule, "Always barf in the bag provided."

A lot of my anxiousness comes, I think, from the fundamental lack of control that is part-and-parcel of the whole "being a tiny, flawed human in a massive, unfeeling universe" thing. It's overwhelming knowing that almost everything that happens in the world is completely beyond my control, and when I get overwhelmed I freak out and stress-Google. While I haven't got rid of my anxiety for good (as my therapist says, I'm me, after all), I have a better handle on it these days. When I look down a staircase and think, "If I fall down these I'll be concussed, probably break a leg or two," I'm now also capable of thinking, "Haha, okay, relax Mon." When I start a "what is the universe expanding into and what if when I die the particles in my body are reused to form a Nazi" spiral, I run a bath. It's not going to solve any of the world's larger problems, but it feels pretty damn good. And that's close enough, for now.

A Poem About Body Image

once
in high school
i drew my body
on some paper
and wrote a list
of all
the flaws i saw

one of the flaws
was
"dumb hands"

i mean

what.

3

WERK

Getting A Job,
A Story By Your Parents

❦

You rise early, despite having gone to sleep late at 10 PM the night before. "Good morning, world!" you, their sweet daughter who they love and cherish, so talented the world is your frickin' oyster, shout out your window as morning radio plays in the background. The world mirrors your enthusiasm.

You pick out a sensible outfit: a pair of slacks (everyone calls them slacks, that's what they're called) and a blazer with that kicky blouse your mom got you. She's very thoughtful, and the blouse is a perfect balance of professional and fun, because you artsy types like to be a bit different and she knows that. She gets you.

You eat a balanced breakfast because you were listening when a very wise *someone* told you that was important. You make sure to drink some milk, because of your bones. You double-check that the oven is turned off, lock your front door, then head out into the world with the air of a soon-to-be Employed Person. Today you're going to knock on some doors.

Heading into the city's neatly delineated, easy-to-define "downtown" area, you think to yourself, *glad I'm not here at night and will be able to take the subway home before dark.* You're Danger Aware. You're also packing a hot Duo-tang full of printed resumes that do NOT include your Twitter handle because why would that be necessary? You are a Bachelor of the Humanities. You deserve this.

The first door you knock on is that of a Business Office. Everyone inside looks very respectable and stressed. They are thinking about their families and drinking coffee and one guy is making such a good joke, oh my god you should hear this joke, you wouldn't believe it, he should be a comedian. Later when you try to tell the joke to your friends you will get lost somewhere around "so the duck says to the chicken," go silent for a bit, and then just leave it. That's fine.

You're not sure where in The Office to go, so you ask the receptionist for help. She is young (forty) like you (twenty-three) so she gets what you're going through. "Nice blazer," she says, genuinely impressed. "Very work appropriate." Everyone around you is wearing a blazer. This blazer is the best purchase you have ever made. The job is basically in the bag. "I've never smoked pot and there are no pictures of me drinking on Facebook," you tell her. She looks like she might pass out.

Regaining her composure, she leads you to an area marked "Interview Space." "We're basically always hiring," she says. "It's so weird to me how few people go out knocking on doors. They just don't know what's out there!" You wait for a while and read exciting magazine articles about the warming planet. You're not worried, and you're not mad at your parents or their friends or the system. You're not even thinking about sexting, which is what's been holding you back from lucrative employment this entire time. Between thinking up clever hashtags, doing selfies, and photographing your genitals for just whoever, you haven't had time to get a job. You're not mad at yourself, just disappointed.

To pass some time in the waiting room you read an article about youth culture in the *New York Times*. It's like looking in a mirror.

Finally, the Boss comes out of her office. "Right this way," *she* says. She is also wearing a blazer, but you can tell hers is of a better quality. She probably listened to her mother when she said that it makes more sense to spend money on fewer items of clothing that are better made. Inside her office are the hallmarks of the life you want: a novelty mug, photos of her kids doing various activities requiring an upper-middle-class income, a motivational poster (advertisement for mortgages), and a landline.

"Great resume," the lady boss begins. "Thanks!" you say, politely. You feel good because manners are their own reward. "And you're on LinkedIn," she says. "That's good, *very* good. We can't hire anyone these days without a LinkedIn profile." You're killing this. Could you *be* any more prepared? (That's a reference to popular Matthew Parrish character Charnler Bing, from the show with the couch.)

"Wow, a university degree?" She raises her eyebrows, blazer-level impressed, and makes some notes on her pad. "English language *and* literature? You might be over-qualified… " You hold back on telling her about your minor in Roman history, lest she be overwhelmed. In a gesture of extreme interest, your future boss Leans In. She looks over your extracurriculars, tutting thoughtfully as she pictures the contributions such a talented amateur canoeist might make in a corporate setting.

The interview is zipping along nicely when you hit a snag. "It says here you stopped taking science in tenth grade," the boss says, flipping through her detailed notes. "Why'd you shut that door?" You don't have a good answer. You should have continued taking science, and you know it. "Mostly, I'm just eager to learn, and ready to do whatever you need. I'm not afraid to get my hands dirty, and I work well independently and as part of a team," you say, with a poise and intelligence suggestive of a person who could have easily passed eleventh-grade science if only they'd applied themselves. The interviewer smiles.

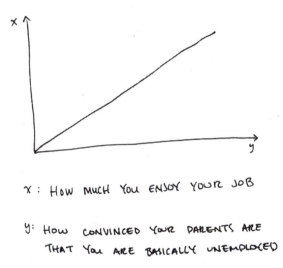

x : How much you enjoy your job

y: How convinced your parents are that you are basically unemployed

"Well, of course you can have the job. All we're ever looking for is a motivated self-starter who's willing to take initiative," she says. Normally, your millennial hands would be straining at the fingertips to avoid tweeting your good news, but even the sweet allure of Tweeter can't pull you away from the joy you feel at this new position. "It's a competitive salary, with full benefits, obviously, and a pension and full-time hours. You know, a job! That's what a job is."

After a quick handshake and a signed contract (which you read in its entirety), your new status as an employed person is secure. You're heading out into the sunshine—putting your headphones in before you're even out the door, that is so you— when the boss lady's voice stops you in the hall. "Hey kid," she says. "I think you'll be needing this." She takes off her blazer and throws it to you. "See you Monday. Wear that scarf your mother got you, it looks so good with your hair."

Should You Get Business Cards

❧

A Quiz

I recently attended a party. As I was leaving, a new acquaintance asked, "Can I have your card?"

The point of that riveting anecdote is twofold: I told it to a) brag that I've been to a party and b) freak out because I do not have a business card card and really can't tell whether or not having one would be helpful for me, oh god, I'm so nervous. Do you have one? Do you use it? What does it look like? Where did you get it? Everyone please mail me your business cards so I can look at them all and think about this Important Issue. While the card-havers are looking for stamps, let's us non-cardholders take a gentle, calming quiz to see if our lives are in need of them. There we go. Nothing to be scared of. Just a nice quiz.

As a starting point, you are:

a. The sole proprietor of a small, independent business with a lot of heart but also a lot of overheads.

b. A naughty duke with a naughty smile and even naughtier past.

c. The worst guy at a dinner party.

d. A vanilla-scented wisp of feminine energy with a retro vibe.

Your business card would likely contain the following information:

a. The details of your business, plus website, Twitter handle and phone number.

b. The first clue in a set of cryptic directions to your underground pleasure garden.

c. "Dreamer. Seeker. Proud Dad. Amateur Potter."

d. A self-effacing story about the time you fell on the ground and your crush saw.

Your card will be made of:

a. Um, paper.

b. The stolen undergarments of the Pemberley sisters.

c. Regular paper but you refer to it as "eco-fabric" because it's made of trees, like all paper.

d. Oh, you're gonna knit it. Don't even front like you're not going to knit it, because you are.

Your business card would in theory be used to:

a. Legitimize your work in the eyes of your parents.

b. Call upon widows at home.

c. Suggest that someone "liaise" with you so you can "connect" at your "upcoming networking event."

d. Make an origami bird to leave on the windowsill of someone having a bad day. It's fun to do nice things for others!

You would actually use it most often to:
a. Efficiently give your contact information to interested parties.
b. Deliver sexual papercuts.
c. Cut mad lines (drug lines) for you (a drug user) and your banker friends (who love drugs).
d. Record lyrics for your adorable ukulele Vine songs.

When handing out your card you're going to say:
a. "Looking forward to hearing from you."
b. "Till we meet again, Elizabeth."
c. "Wicked, sick. Hit me up on Snapchat, man. Hashtag PARTY, am I right??"
d. You won't be able to say anything because you'll have tripped over your tiny feet trying to stand up in an authoritative way.

Mostly A's
It sounds like you are trying to make an honest living at the helm of a small business you believe in. Why not get business cards, I guess? (cc: THIS ECONOMY.)

Mostly B's
You are a cad and a rogue and possibly a nineteenth-century lord. You should get business cards but stay away from the Pemberley sisters, they're good girls.

Mostly C's
No one wants your business card.

Mostly D's
You are Zooey Deschanel and do not need a business card.

Working From Home: How To Do It

❧

If there's one thing to be said for the paucity of traditional jobs with regular hours and benefits and the like, it's that there is now no shortage of underpaid, underwhelming positions that allow you to work from home in your underwear. Sure, none of us have any job security and I can't even spell penison, but I certainly do get to set my own hours and work from a crowded coffee shop or comfy couch of my choosing!

Although while the home office is free of many hazards of a professional workplace, it poses its own unique challenges, chief among them time management. How to keep working with no boss looking over your shoulder? How to meet deadlines with so many episodes of *House of Cards* just waiting for you on Netflix? How to stay on task when the whole Internet is right there, waiting to be read, liked, and masturbated to? Let's discuss:

Figure Out Your Ideal Working Conditions
Do you need lots of natural light or a specific productivity playlist or an espresso constantly at the ready? Whatever you need to do

to get going—get dressed like a real person, start the day with a big breakfast, make an incredibly precise to-do list, don your power kimono—is what you should do. Just because you don't have the routine of going into an office doesn't mean you can't have a getting ready for work routine at home. Make a cup of tea, check some emails and head to your workspace to get cracking.

Try to Own at Least One Outfit You Could Describe as "Not a Kimono"

I get it. Sweatpants are comfortable, bras are not. An open robe allows you to be simultaneously naked *and* clothed *and* involved in solo *Game of Thrones* cosplay. But it's vital that you own the kinds of clothes you've seen other adult humans wear, in the street or on TV. Consider: pants with a zipper. A skirt! They are making a ton of fun knitwear these days. You have options that are not perilously tied at the front. Use them.

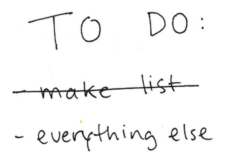

Don't Compare Yourself to Others

Not everyone is an early riser, and there's nothing wrong with needing a break in the middle of the day or at any other time. Sure, your friend who works from home rises with the sun and does two hours of yoga before growing her own breakfast and sitting down to write her novel, but that's not you and it won't ever be. Wake up when it works for you and work how you need to work.

Develop a Routine and Stick to It

It takes thirty days to form a habit, and approximately two-to-six weeks for this amazing kimono designer to ship custom creations straight to your door. Try to divide your time reasonably between working, sending furious emails about how quickly your new kimono will arrive, and tending to any tasks related to home life that may arise. By setting a daily schedule, you'll get more work done, and have more time for online kimono shopping.

Take Things One Day at a Time

Set micro-deadlines and small goals to accomplish each day. That way you know what you need to get done and can end your day when you complete those tasks, even if the overall job you're working on is far from finished. Tomorrow you can do more! Working from home shouldn't mean never escaping your job.

Swanning Around Your Apartment in an Elegant Vintage Kimono That You Got on a Super Amazing Sale is Not the Same as Accomplishing Anything, You Need to Start Taking Your Life More Seriously, Monica, I Mean It

I don't know you and you don't know me so this is just one of a number of helpful tips to increase your and my productivity, and it could certainly apply to anyone. A tip to whoever out there is struggling with this issue: if you don't start wearing a bra under the kimono, one day your neighbours are going to see

your boobs. Probably. I mean, it just seems like a likely scenario. For a stranger.

Keep in Contact w/ the Outside World
Just because you can work in your pajamas doesn't mean you can sleep through emails/calls from clients or a boss of some kind. It's also helpful to check in with friends or family who work more regular jobs, to avoid feeling like a lonely cave-dweller trapped at the bottom of the sea while the world floats by above.

Don't Sink All Your Savings into Starting a Kimonos4Freelancers Wholesale Robe Retail Business
I do not need the competition.

Be a Grownup about Time Management
You can't watch porn/play video games/take photos for your kimono portfolio all day long. You can play around with your

schedule a little bit, and you have the freedom of doing it alllll in your underwear if you want to (you want to), but know when you need to buckle down and put together something great, and just do it already. If you start working an hour later than you planned, you should end work an hour later than you intended to, even if that means not slipping out of your house kimono into your going out kimono until 6 PM instead of 5 PM like you planned.

Would You Like to Buy a Kimono?

We also carry shortie robes, terrycloth options, wizard garb, and swaddling silks. It's, uh, important... for working. From home. I'm a professional.

Some Suggestions For Your Dream Job

❋

There are some very good jobs out there. At least a few people in the world wake up every day thinking, "I wonder how tiny and hungry for love the baby otter I have to carefully nurse back to health will be *this time?*" It's also someone's job to oil the supple butts of our favourite celebrities for their controversial butt-reveal magazine covers. Many women and indeed, some men, are living the indie romcom dream of waking up early to run their urban cupcake shoppes, with those extra P's and E's and everything. Still, there are other jobs out there. Other jobs that should—and could?—be real. Jobs I would like to have. So far they don't exist. But someday. Someday...

Avocado Fairy

The thing that seems most appealing about public service jobs—barista, Sinter Klaus, sandwich artist—is that you're giving people something they really need. Of course, people are ungrateful bastards, and as any former barista can tell you (hi), there's very little goodwill to be felt for your customers when they're screaming at you for giving them 1% instead of skim or for not hearing when they asked for "extra whip" (they did not ask but you can't argue). An Avocado Fairy would be that rare gem: a service job that people actually appreciate. Swooping into clients' homes the *moment* their avocados are usably ripe so they'll never be stuck with a sub-par guac or jump the gun on some hard 'cados again. Bliss.

Historical Reenactor: Bacchanal Division
Clinging togas. Opulent feasts. Barrels of fine wine. Uninhibited, anything-goes group sex till dawn. A regular paycheque. Because I love and respect The Past.

Library Shusher
Silence in the library is something I'm very passionate about, along with turning all the lights on at the end of a party and raining on parades. Librarians are often far too busy with computers and cataloging and low-budget pornography to carry out the requisite shushing needed to keep a library exquisitely silent, like a smart people tomb. This is where I come in. With a strong index finger from hours of texting and judgemental pointing, and a strong diaphragm from speaking at approximately two to three times the appropriate volume for a Bus Conversation, I'm kind of an ideal candidate. Now SHHH.

Internet Humour Writer
It feels real, but my tax return is like, "girl please."

Plant Therapist

I come into your home and give your green life the love and care
it deserves. The green life does not judge my singing (or dancing)
and as long as I water it we get along just fine. You come home
to a house just poppin' with O_2 and pay me thousands if not
millions of dollars. I leave, having pocketed one tiny succulent
as a tip. The plants wave goodbye.

Ice Cream Pope

Cookie dough miracles, rocky road benedictions... basically I'm
picturing a waffle cone mitre and that's where this fantasy ends.

Netflix Experience Quality Evaluator

Customer experience surveys simply aren't reliable—after
hours of *Homeland*, people will say anything. That's why it
would be my duty to pop Netflix on from nine to five, and offer
important suggestions for improvement like "should come with
snacks," "why does mine keep suggesting Female Leads With
Food Problems," and "please make a category for films with
many exposed dongs, did I mention snacks are essential?"

Sext Consultant

See page 214.

Compliments Tester

I have a good ear for compliments. I can really tell when
someone means it. Test all your well-intentioned bon mots on
me before depositing them on your girlfriends, besties, moms,
cats, whoever. Note: I have a highly developed backhanded-ness
detector from years of theatre school.

Technology Accident Consolation Manager

Drop your phone in the toilet again? I'm so, so sorry. That really sucks. I have rice in my purse and I'll compose an appropriately self-effacing "contact me via email" status update so your friends are informed. Sit on your computer and can't afford a new one? Here, punch this pillow. Punch it as hard as you want, it's not going to break. Not like your computer! Just a bit of levity there, to get you through this difficult moment. I'm a professional.

Siren

Either a human version of the loud noise coming from ambulances and firetrucks, or a half-woman half-fish creature that lures sailors to a rocky death, I'm not picky.

A Poem About The Shared Fridge At Work

❋

This is just to say

I have eaten
the pizza
that was in
the fridge

and which
you were probably
saving
to eat later.

I regret nothing.

An Introduction To Some Difficult Workplace Truths

"Team building activities" are just another word for "being embarrassed in a polo shirt."

You will never, ever, successfully "take an outfit from work to cocktails" with the removal or addition of a blazer.

If you are an intern, your entire job is to look busy and be silent. Anything you attempt to do for regular employees is probably unhelpful and almost certainly annoying. Just quietly flirt with the other interns and collect your school credit at the end.

Your entire employment period is basically a countdown to accidentally calling your supervisor "Mom" in front of everyone.

That little cough you do in the bathroom is fooling no one.

There will be colleagues for whom you will miss the Acceptable Ask threshold, name-wise. Avoid embarrassment by calling everyone you work with "Paul." You are bound to be right at least some of the time.

No one actually hangs out by the water cooler. It is, however, a great place to go to be alone.

Under no circumstance should you tell your colleagues about your creative ambitions. Cruelty, thy name is Howard from HR showing up at your poetry reading with thoughts on your "evocative similes."

Everyone hates your novelty mug.

Nothing is certain but death, taxes, and the fact that you will someday hit "reply all" when you should not have hit "reply all."

Your coworkers aged forty and up are confused about your sexuality.

You have to buy the thing Frank's kid is selling. There's no way around it. At least get a charity receipt.

There is no such thing as a flattering beige work pant.

You're going to have more than "one or two" glasses of wine at the Christmas party. You are going to tell Donna from Accounting your Secrets.

Bringing your lunch from home just means you will spend money on a second lunch at 2 PM.

You should not try to get funky with your office attire. You can express yourself through fashion when you are sixty-five, have saved well, and are happily poolside in your Retirement Caftan.

No matter how disguised your real name is, your colleagues WILL find you on Facebook.

The words "business casual" are a trap.

SHOOT FOR THE MOON. EVEN IF YOU MISS, YOU'LL BE IMMEDIATELY TORN APART BY THE UNFEELING VACUUM OF SPACE.

How To Handle Getting Fired

❧

Like flared jeans or smoking the wrong kind of drugs by accident, getting fired is an unpleasant though not life-ruining occurrence that most of us will experience at some point in our teens or twenties. Whether you've been made redundant, come in hungover one too many times, keep calling the kids you're teaching "assholes" or are being replaced by a robot in this fast-paced, technology-driven world, do not fret. Being fired, because of its finality, is actually a lot simpler to deal with than theoretically smaller office disputes like communal dish washing practice or who keeps turning the A/C up even though everyone is wearing sweaters inside in July and do you have incredibly sensitive nipples, Barry, or do you just hate the Earth?? Here's how to find out you're being offered "indefinite unpaid leave with the option to pursue new employment" like a boss:

See It Coming

Be honest: how good are you at your job? How much does your boss like you? How often do you live up to all your promises to be a team player ready at any moment to lead when necessary? When was the last time you laughed meaningfully at that "Hang In There" poster above your cubicle? Why didn't you come to all-team bowling the other night? If you're anything like me, you were a great employee for about six hot weeks, then became exponentially worse as your employment period dragged on. At this point you are basically a comedy teen in an '80s movie, that is how bad you are at your job. Just know the comedy teen usually gets fired.

Really Make the Most of Your Last Week

If you feel like you're getting the axe soon (or know it through company gossip, a leaked memo, or *TMZ*), why not live it up? Steal some pens, come in late, flirt with your supervisor. It's hard to use a place that fired you as reference for further jobs anyway, and besides: free pens are one of corporate life's greatest pleasures. Send a ton of chain letter forwards ("If YoU sToP rEaDiNg ThIs YoU'lL dIe SoMeDaY"), change your Twitter bio to read "opinions ONLY my employer's," wear jeans on a Monday. Who cares, you're a dead man walking. Eat your last meal (a tuna melt) in your boss's doorway. Really let those aromas waft.

Consider Your Options

Basically, if there is severance involved, do not quit. If there is not, maybe give your notice! Then you aren't technically fired, and can pretend this is some kind of very public high-stakes decision where you were "given the option" and chose to leave with your head held high. If you're feeling a change in the wind, so to speak (not a fart joke), start poking around for upcoming employment opportunities elsewhere (fart joke writer?). Put feelers out with friends who have jobs at places you might like to work, check job postings, beg your parents to help get you hired somewhere because Sarah's mom works at Google and she rides a company Segway to work every day, etc.

Obligatory Though Grim Step: Consider Briefly the Selling of Your Underwear and Other Intimate Items for Unbelievably Small Amounts of Money on Craigslist

An important step in accepting your pending unemployment is the night you spend reading CL ads and wondering if maybe "topless cleaner, must jiggle while vacuuming" might not be so terrible a gig after all. This period is almost always cut short when the sheer amount of effort and time required to a) buy b) soil c) sell and d) deliver one's underwear to anonymous Internet perverts is revealed to yield about $20 per pair, if you're lucky.

Make Them Suffer

The big boss at a company is like the big boss in a video game: scariest guy on the level, weird monster face, best defeated by cunning. If you're heading in for what feels like your Last Day, wear something innocent and angelic. Play up your youth with a backpack covered in pins you got at pop punk concerts. Play up your innocence by wearing something you last wore to school picture day 1999. Wear very bad quality mascara so that when the axe is raised and you raise your weepy eyes to the heavens, your face is a veritable swamp of tears. As you leave the room, take one final look back and say, "You know, I've always thought of you as a parent. Thank you for all that you've taught me," then limp out the door. Fin.

Picture Your Boss as Donald Trump Doing That Heavy-Lidded, Floppy-Haired, Mouth-so-Pursed-it-Looks-like-a-Butt Face

"You're fired." Whatever you say, buttmouth.

Move On with Grace

It's probably not worth it to scorch the Earth in your exit... unless you have a very good swear word to yell as the elevator doors close.

4

It's Called Manners, Read a Book

When It's Time To Switch To Water

You've suddenly discovered that you've had too much to drink. If you know this because you realized it yourself, congratulations! You have caught yourself early and can help yourself without involving others. Calmly proceed to the nearest tap and avail yourself of a glass or two of Sweet Lady H_2O. If you know this because it was just told to you tactfully and quietly by an outside source, please remember something, and I need you to listen to me here: no one is patronizing you. Having spent my share of loud, hungry hours in university as a fairly dedicated Weekend Drunk Girl, I can tell you for a fact that being patronized is the Drunk Girl's No. 1 greatest fear and she needs to chill out, take a sip of water, and stop being confrontational with her boyfriend about it. (Sorry, Paul.) Here are some other signs it's time to make like a fan of 1990s Danish-Norwegian pop supergroup and love on some AQUA.

You're Having Large-Scale Purse Problems

"I think someone stole my purse… it's not in the pile near the door where I left it. I bet it was that girl over there. No, HER. Not her, her. HER, I SAID. Yeah, the bartender. She wanted it. I know she wanted it. It's a nice one. It matches this one I have… oh, I'm wearing it. I think someone stole my wallet. Stop judging me right now, you're judging me." Get some water!

You Think Someone "Hates You" And You Want to Ask Them about It at Length

No one hates you. They might, though, if you keep asking them whether or not they do! Get some water.

One Or Both of Your Nipples Have Been Seen by One Or More People at The Party, Not on Purpose

Whether you winked a boob at an unsuspecting potential paramour or your dress has shifted throughout the night to reveal a whisper of areola, if your sweaterpuppies have become unsweatered, it's time to get some water.

You Like, Really Want McDonald's

No part of a McDonald's cheeseburger—not the bun, not the burger, not the cheez—looks or tastes anything like the thing it is supposed to be. And yet, good LORD, pop a bite of that ketchup—and pickle-laden junk on my tongue at 3 AM and I am in Drunk Girl Heaven. ("If you have both your shoes you're not allowed in."—Drunk St. Paul at the gates to Drunk Heaven) It is not good for you and it makes hangovers infinitely worse. Get a water, go home and have a life-reviving sandwich.

You Are Considering Peeing Somewhere That is Not a Bathroom

Do not do this. Locate a bathroom, then get some water.

Did You Just Try to Get Someone to Kiss You Using Trickery?

If you have to prank someone into touching their mouth to your mouth, they don't want to kiss you and you are being a sex pest. *Get some water!* I know it's time for me to get some water when I start doing "My Move," which is literally just staring at some poor human "in a sexy way" until they either a) get uncomfortable and leave my field of vision, or b) come over because they're intrigued (and/or worried I have possibly had a stroke). I never "get some" with this move. But I do get some water.

"I Only Smoke When I'm Drinking"

You smell like a sad Grandpa. Get some water.

Other Miscellaneous (but important) Signs it's Time to Switch to Water:

You are crying; you are yelling; you are eating at a speed you find uncomfortable; you are telling your family's secrets; you're trying to use your phone and it just... isn't... happening; you are trying to use your phone and it is happening, and what is happening is that you are calling Spain; you are bleeding from the hand; you are threatening to fight someone; you are sleepy; you're having irresponsible sext; you are being a li'l brat to the person you have a crush on; you stepped in someone else's puke and you're not sure how it's going to go for you, puke-wise; you are bringing up that thing your partner did that time and trying to fight them about it; you are thirsty, for water.

As no one cool has ever said (until NOW?): there's no shame in getting some water. Sip it up, apologize to the bartender about the purse thing, and you're good to go.

Good Mistakes vs. Bad Mistakes: A Fuck Up's Guide

❧

There is nothing wrong with making mistakes. We know this. It's important to forgive yourself when you mess up, because life is full of messes. Making poor decisions or not having things work out can be a helpful learning experience, or at least the set up to a fun anecdote you can deploy to seem breezy at job interviews. But not all mistakes are created equal. There's "ha ha, whoops!" and "ha ha, whoops! Sorry about your dog, but I guess it was pretty old anyways!" In case you're worried you're in danger of making a bad mistake instead of a good one, here's an incomplete list of good versus bad fuck ups.

Good mistakes: night cheese; dresses with unnecessary and salacious cut-outs; putting yourself out there even though it turned out very embarrassing; trying a new food only to discover you are not really ready for the vegan lifestyle; leaving your phone at home; basically anything you chose to wear in the early 2000s; persevering with your dream of having tiny, Bettie Page-style babybangs in the face of longstanding and increasingly

100

intense protest from your friends and loved ones; pizza for one; telling your adult friends your childhood nickname; the "69" sexual position; trying stand-up comedy just once, why not; letting your fanciest friend pick the dinner place; funny tattoos but only if they are legitimately very funny; online shopping after 3 AM; forgetting to order a salad instead of fries; risky-yet-romantic travel gestures; teenage poetry; really giving it 110% at karaoke; flaking on your friends to sleep for a bit instead; cutting up your camp T-shirt to "make it your own;" being overdressed; trying to speak French to a French person; more or less whatever you do that turns out poorly but also makes you laugh or learn (TM a framed poster in a sorority).

Bad mistakes: unprotected sex with strangers; capri pants; getting too intense about bicycles; doing something "so you can write about it later;" being quietly jealous of a cool girl instead of friending the shit out of her; renting an apartment without seeing it in person first; that crystal deodorant that's actually just a useless crystal; " Googling your symptoms; flared jeans; travelling with your family for more than five to seven days maximum; letting your boss talk down to you; doing a juice cleanse; live music; trying to be "just one of the guys;" telling anyone about your juice cleanse; keeping your phone on any setting other than silent; creeping too deep on Instagram, Facebook, Twitter, or in real life; most of the people you will date before age twenty-five; texting after 3 AM or five or more drinks; asking someone if they are pregnant, why would you do that, just why; your "punk" phase, almost always; that last drink "for the road;" hats; presuming everyone is talking about you, I promise they're not; basically anything that makes you feel yucky in your gut or heart.

Some Notes On Etiquette For The Behaviourally Disenfranchised

Eye contact on the subway is just as unwelcome as thigh contact on the subway. Refrain from any kind of contact on the subway.

Of course your friend is not more interesting than the entire Internet, but it is polite to keep up the illusion that you'd rather converse with a real human than scroll through a database containing thousands of pictures of animals who are friends. (Put down your phone.)

No one wants to hear about your screenplay.

Texting "U up?" at 3 AM assumes that the state of being awake is tantamount to desiring your body. This is presumptuous. Please be more descriptive in your inquiry.

We do not all need to stop and talk when we run into each other on the street. For the love of God, a nod will suffice.

A gentleman never screengrabs.

The coolest way to respond to a fart is by saying nothing at all. That conspiratorial face you are making at the other guy in the elevator is completely selling out your flatulent coworker. Stand down. You are not the Fart Police.

Mentioning someone's web presence IRL is the Elephant Graveyard of conversation topics: you must never go there.

Your cat is very cute, but please calm down.

There is no less sexy time than the moments spent in a romantic conquest's apartment prior to the arrival of Night Pizza.

If your friend's boyfriend or girlfriend is terrible, it is a matter of good manners to gently inform her of this. Life is too short to date people who play in cover bands.

Treat others how you would like to be treated, even if you know for sure that they swiped left.

The proper protocol upon seeing an adult human engaged in targeted winking is a Citizen's Arrest.

True friends are there for each other's Instagram B-sides. Lowlight landscapes and filter missteps (Nashville, I'm looking at you) don't matter; this is about supporting your friend as an artist.

No one thinks your opinions represent those of your employer, so you can probably relax about this.

It is your duty to inform everyone at the party if there is marijuana in the food.

Alerting a person to the fact that they are on speakerphone as quickly as possible is a Sacred Trust.

If you "favourite" three or more of a person's tweets in a row, or any of their tweets after 3 AM, you are legally considered "too thirsty for this Earth" and should check yourself into Horny Jail.

In break ups, obey the words of contemporary sage Miley Cyrus: "When you mean it / I'll believe it / If you text it / I'll delete it."

No matter how good your news is, the rest of the bus will be mad at you for talking on the phone about it.

Two exclamation marks in a work email is polite and upbeat. More than three makes you seem a danger to yourself and others.

A true lady hides her real-life misandry in upbeat, web-based humour.

Faving without following is cheeky as hell. Pick a side.

Your parents deserve the truth. Repeat after me: "Mom, the reason you cannot look at my phone is because at this point, it's a library of pictures of different naked people."

Alanis knew not all the lyrics were ironic and that is what makes the song itself ironic. Retire this topic of discussion.

EXCUSE ME SIR:
PLEASE
STOP TALKING TO ME
ABOUT YOUR BAND

"GET OUT OF CONVERSATIONAL JAIL FREE" CARD

How To Survive Your
Family's Holiday Party

❧

It's 10 AM on December 25th and seriously, Mom, do we have to go to that thing at Aunt Linda's house? Can't we just do brunch and get Christmas drunk on mimosas, watch It's a Wonderful Life and fall asleep in our new pajamas? No? Okay, fine. But I'm positioning myself firmly by the shrimp and if anyone tries to move me, toddler or no, they are getting a mean face and an overly-involved story about a recent revelation regarding my gynecological health. What is it about the melting pot of personalities, relationships, and different takes on what "gravy" means that makes hanging with your family at Christmas or any other holiday such a mince pie minefield?

I really enjoy the company of my extended family. My dad's side knows that all you need to make a sandwich is gravy and bread, and all the women on my mom's side think they are psychic which is obviously wonderful. But whether or not your aunties, grandpas, and a million confusing combinations of second and third cousins twice removed (we all have giant

Catholic families from PEI, right?) are your favourite people in the world, the holidays can be tricky, socially. What do you bring? How much do you drink? What amount of info about your personal life do you really need to tell people you only see a few times a year? What do you do if your grandma gets drunk and starts reminiscing about necking in the back of a car in the '40s? What if one of your relatives is getting really aggressive about his bullshit conservative politics? Don't worry, friends. You've got this.

Eat and Drink Up

This is some of the nicest food you will eat all year—what, you're making stuffing from scratch casually in your daily life?—and your older relatives probably won't even let you help with the dishes. Cheese platter, *ho!* (I mean that like the way pirates shout upon seeing land, but it's also pretty perfect as an imperative. Bacon-wrapped shrimp, hos!) This is also some of the nicest wine and/or beer and/or fancy spirits that you're likely to encounter for a while, so get in there. Family drunk is a sacred, beautiful thing. Just don't overdo it; last year I got so accidentally boozy on mimosas I had to go upstairs and Secret Nap for a bit.

Miss Manners

Do the manners thing, you guys. If only to dampen some of the "kids these days" arguments that are floating around. Turn off your phone for a bit and participate in a lovely tradition that's been happening as long as humans have existed: shared food and group yelling. Don't worry about gifts but do BE PRESENT, you know? (You can use that line whenever, it's appropriate on birthdays too, so, you're welcome.) If you have to be an asshole the rest of the year, please remember that this is the one night when please and thank yous and not texting while someone is talking to you are really important. You can go back to cutting in line to order coffee while talking too loudly on your cellphone and planning to eat your malodorous sandwich on a crowded bus in rush hour tomorrow, you grinch. Offer to help, bring a food or drink, be someone's designated driver or accompany them on a walk home. Be tactful if someone goes on a political, religious, or moral rant that you don't agree with. Do you really need to pick a fight with your elderly relative over politics on Hanukkah? What will it achieve? Try to move the conversation away to something nicer, like bread rolls, or different types of trees (balsam is a personal favourite, if you're looking for a hard line to draw). You can do this.

Don't Bring Your Significant Other Unless They Are Here2Stay

If you only see your extended family once a year, be warned: they will ask about that nice young man or woman you brought last year for EVER until you bring another one. This is just them being polite and working with what little they know about you, which might just be your name (or at least a name similar to yours. I accept "Marnie," "Melissa," and "Michael" at family functions). Your first Christmas on your own after a break up is going to be a triple nightmare with well-meaning cousins saying things like "Soooo, how are things with Lauren?" This may or may not lead to a three-sherry phone error starring the slurred phrase, "I just don't know what happened, Lauren," which is obviously something we'd all like to avoid. Lauren especially.

Join In When the Older Aunties Start Playing the Spoons and Dancing
#PEI

Place to Be: The Kids Table
Man, kids that aren't your problem are fun. They have almost no filter and the good ones do not put their jam-hands on you without asking. They will say hilarious things that are mean and nice all at the same time, e.g. "You're very pretty like Cinderella except you have silly orange hair." They might even tell you secrets about your relatives aka their parents. There are worse ways to spend an hour or two than feeding shortbread to a new doll with a four-year-old. Although these days it's probably some interactive hologram-doll running off an iPad that the four-year-old has hacked to play "Let It Go" from *Frozen* in the background of a virtual tea party while you were busy trying to figure out how to turn off the flash on your phone like some kind of elderly troglodyte. Children are the future, etc. etc.

Or, Get to Know the Olds
If children are the future, your grandparents and great-grandparents are the past in present. My mom's dad went from living on a farm in Prince Edward Island to fighting in WWII to driving a car and owning a cellphone. Plus, he was hilarious and had a million great stories. Old people are living history, have way less of a filter than anyone under sixty, and are way cooler than they sometimes get credit for. Your grandma, for instance, is a non-meme Betty White just waiting to tell you about being a woman on a mostly male university campus in the '30s or the year she spent living in Africa. Old people are smart, storied,

hilarious, and not to get all wah-wahh on you, but they're not gonna be here forever. Put in some face time with the lovely people who keep you in sweaters. They'll appreciate it too.

Be Grateful, You Scrooge!

Not everyone has a family they are close with. Not everyone has a family, period. Consider, some people out there who don't even know you all that well actually think you are important enough to have over to their home for a meal, a meal that took a long time to cook, so that everyone can celebrate what's happened this year and what may happen in the next. Get over yourself and have a nice time. It's a PARTY.

As usual, most of this advice boils down to "don't be a jerk." Instead, try to do positive things for yourself and others. Have a very lovely holiday and try not to worry too much about how the winters are getting warmer every year and what are we even going to DO about the song "White Christmas" when that doesn't make sense as a thing anymore? Enjoy your family dinner/pagan ceremony/low-key movie and Chinese food, however and whatever you choose to do. Also, everyone be cool about the five pounds you may or may not gain; consider it prudent winter insulation.

An Incomplete List Of Things That Are Rude

❁

Low-rise jeans
The word "Ma'am"
Unexpected raisins
Facebook messenger
Cats
Group texts
Low-fat cheese
The word "Miss"
Excessive rain
Any wind

Taylor Swift's legs

Low-rise jeans, whose idea were those

The premise of Tinder

Turtlenecks

Ribbed Turtlenecks

Confronting someone about why they unfollowed
you on Twitter

The "Reply All" button

Temporary tattoos that will NOT come off

Low-rise jeans, though, right?

The phrase, "You look tired"

Swans

The sun

Your phone's front-facing camera turning on
unexpectedly at a low angle

Periods

Internet comments

Low chairs

The phrase, "Calm down"

Vanity sizing

Mandatory group bonding exercises

People who make you sing when you're just trying to
do improv and go home

Mom burns (the truest burns)

Taking forever to text back, we're all on our phones always,
I see you

Just texting back "k," like what is that about

Visible Panty Line

Pointing out someone's Visible Panty Line, what are you,
twelve?

The phrase "TL;DR"
Inviting someone to your comedy show face-to-face
so they can't say no
Phones that aren't waterproof
Tripping hazards
The Dutch
"Let's just split the bill three ways"
Cold tampons
Leftovers you forgot about a day too long
Value-Added Tax
Compliments from your enemies
Changing the channel when someone is just trying to
watch the goddamn Food Network in peace
Did I say low-rise jeans, because good God

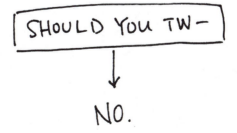

Should You Text Them Back?

❋

A Quiz

What time is it?

a. 9 PM on a Friday.

b. 7 AM on a Sunday.

c. Noon on a Wednesday.

d. 3 AM on a Tuesday.

What's the message?

a. "If I could change the alphabet I'd put Pi and Zza together."

b. "Hi sweetie want to meet for breakfast this morning hope you weren't up 2late lol love dad."

c. "It's your LUCKY DAY Text 186969 To This Number And You're Entered To Win A Free CRUISE Plus Gold-Plated Dog For All Your Glistening Companion Needs!****charges and service charges apply visit website for details but please don't****."

d. "u up?"

Who's it from?
a. Allison, your friend who works at a particularly lax Pizzaville.
b. A number you don't know, but you're… pretty sure it's your dad? You hope it's your dad.
c. [Unlisted]
d. "SHANNON DON'T PICK UP HE'S THE DEVIL."

What are you doing right now?
a. Why does it matter, the answer isn't, "eating pizza"?
b. Sleeping and trying to ignore that it tastes like a cigarette peed in my mouth last night.
c. Yearning for the sea.
d. Watching porn and wondering if I'll die alone.

What are you considering saying back?
a. "I'm not eating carbs right now."
b. Nothing, it's 7 AM on a Sunday.
c. "Please send me more information, this DOES sound like the deal of a lifetime!"
d. "I think about you every day, I'm thinking about you right now, I wish you were a more cautious driver and I miss my dog, but you can't change the past and I also miss US."

What are you *actually* going to say back?
a. "I'm not eating carbs right now… JUST KIDDING, I'm not terrible. See you soon."
b. Nothing, it's 7 AM on a Sunday.
c. Oh, hang on, I looked at their website and I probably won't text back.
d. "haha, yeah. come over? nothing serious, just like, something super low-key would be great."

Mostly A's

This text is rhetorical. Do not respond, simply head to Pizzaville.

Mostly B's

It's your dad. Text him back, he worries.

Mostly C's

This is a spam account and they are not for real offering you a cruise. Do not text back.

Mostly D's

Shannon, you deserve better than this. Do not text back.

An Incomplete Guide To People Who Want To Talk To You About Your Body

❧

You're a grown-ass woman, and regardless of the actual size of your ass, it is very likely that people have talked to you about it. Just like, on the street, or at parties, or at the gym. Just wherever. You've got a bod, and members of our society at large have things to say about it.

And worse, it seems like they juuuuust get to. The other day in an elevator, a woman I see in my apartment building sometimes turned to me and said, "You've lost weight, I think." When she left, my boyfriend was all "!!!!" and I was like, "The tampon commercials are right: being a girl DOES rock!" This woman, incidentally, is very nice and doesn't know me very well, and says this every time I see her regardless of the veracity of the pronouncement. I think she is just trying to give me a little boost for my day, which is lovely in theory but obviously one giant sad cat emoji when you consider that "you look thinner" is, in many people's minds, the nicest thing a girl could hear.

That said, "You look thin," by virtue of its unfortunate status in our society as the Ur-compliment, is kind of a nice option compared to some of the other things people feel completely comfortable rhyming off at me (and basically every woman I know) (and all women, in general). Cat-calling is one version of this, but cataloguing parts, commenting on and judging of women's bodies comes from a variety of sources. Sure, you're getting it from that guy on the street, but it's also coming from well-meaning aunts and judgemental gym teachers and employers and coworkers and that one friend that always has something to say about how your pants are fitting these days and you're just kind of like, "COOL IT, VANESSA, PLEASE."

These are some of the people who want to talk to you about your body:

That One Older Man Who Probably Doesn't Mean Anything Gross But Is Actually Sooooo Grosssss and May or May Not Be Aware

DOES HE KNOW IT?! Good God. This man. Just making all kinds of statements that amount quietly but irreversibly to, "I'm looking at your body and I think things about it." "I like the way that blouse fits," he says with Meaningful Eyes when you come into work in the morning. "You've really grown into your figure, you're a woman now!" he says to your chubby fifteen-year-old face at a Christmas party. "How was your vacation? I bet you drove all the boys on the beach wild in your bathing suit. Now let's get this gynecological exam started." That last one is thankfully made up, but you know what I mean: friends' dads who told me my breasts had gotten bigger during puberty, or the old Subway sandwich guy who noticed that I'd lost a bunch of weight in high school and like, congratulated me on it when I ordered a salad? The thought process of these men is so confusing to me: "I have been looking at this young woman's body and noticed something about it, and it's kind of weird that I noticed, and I think I should tell her. Just so she knows. She should know that I think this. It's important." Whyyyyyyy nooooooo please, no it's not.

Your Bitchy Friend

Buddies who make you feel bad about your body are not your buddies, end of thinkpiece. Everyone's got their own body drama, and we can certainly all relate and share with each other as part of dealing with it. But the second their drama starts to become your drama, that's enough of that. If a pal always has something to add about your "problem areas" or wants to compare waist sizes or something else dumb, you should sit them down for some Oprah-to-Lindsay-level Real Talk. [NB: In some unfortunate cases, this bitchy friend can take the form of one's own family. A truly regrettable circumstance and one that requires the realest of talks at the postest of hastes. Whether family or friend, the person in question will almost always claim their concern stems from love for you and problems with themselves, but you are completely within your rights to kindly ask that they express that love, literally, any other way.]

Guys Who Think It's a Compliment to Tell You That Your Bod Makes Their Dingle Tingle

Not a compliment, really! I've got the Internet. I've seen what's on there with this express purpose and a lot of it is way gross! And also, if you can possibly believe it, sir, I do not judge how much my body is makin' it work based on whether or not I can arouse a lonely, gin-soaked man in a dive-y bar. Your comment about my sweet rack has been immediately deleted from the inbox of my brain to make room for cataloguing and storing all the pictures of sunsets I've been fav-ing on Instagram. #blessed

WHY I'M LATE

25% just really grooving to a particular song

50% EYEBROW PROBLEMS

10% unsuccessful coup

10% relative value of my time compared to yours

5% selfies

Passive-Aggressive Strangers

"You're so great at dressing for your body type," is a personal pet peeve, and something I hear semi-frequently. I'm sure most people don't mean it this way, but it really reads to me as, "It's so wild that you can find stores that not only sell but will also help you hoist yourself into whatever ship's sail has been repurposed into a dress for your crazy bizarre body. That colour is so flattering to your corpse's complexion and I can barely even see your tail!" Come on, guys. "You're a great dresser," is a nice, normal compliment that does not implicate the skinsuit and related muscles/bones/blubber a person was born into and has to live with every day. Aggro strangers seem to especially like commenting on the obvious: "That's a strong roman nose you've got there;" "Holy shit girl, look how big your tits are!" "You're extremely thin! Do you get cold easily?" etc. etc. etc., ad literal nauseam. Attention, chatty Cathys and Carls: if it's the first thing you notice when you look at us, it's something we've already thought about. Probably a lot. Probably we don't need you to bring it up. You just never know! Even if you feel like it's positive. "You've lost weight," for instance: if I haven't, it makes me wonder if I should, and if I have, it reinforces this idea I try very hard to ignore, that I'm more attractive sans ten or fifteen pounds.

It's hard out there for a lady with a human woman's body. I'm going to propose something that sounds kind of restrictive, but which I hope might feel incredibly freeing. Maybe as a general rule, just don't talk about other people's bodies? Like, do you have to? If you think about it, it's a very personal thing and there are, at a guess, between 12 and 47,000 other readily available topics you can talk about instead. Think about it. If someone wants your opinion on their body, they will ask you for it. Otherwise, sports are almost always just happening, somewhere, why not talk about that?

And remember: when it really gets too much, you are completely within your rights to throw manners out the window and issue a stern "Shut the fuck up" to any of the above, but also to: authority figures who think you won't sass back, other people's rude grandmothers, construction worker stereotypes who are really letting the team down and who I bet all the gentleman construction workers are mad at, certain dance teachers, girls a grade above you who aren't wearing bras yet, judge-y doctors, TV in general, and, hopefully, no one else!

A Poem About A Night Out

✿

so much depends
upon

a red wheel
barrow

that a drunk girl
tipped over

to use
as a sled.

Leaving A Party, A Gentle How-To

❃

I am not a killjoy, okay? I love a party. ("I'm not a killjoy, I love a party"—the words of someone who is, at best, fine with a party but is not breaking any records for enthusiasm.) I love getting dressed up, I love seeing friends and meeting new people, I *really* love fingerfood. In short, I love a party. But I do not love the general "how dare you" vibes that exist around leaving a party early. People get testy about it, whether you're taking your leave solo or with a crowd, to go somewhere else, or because your shoes broke and you're just not feeling it right now. This is bunk and you should be able to leave even the most rockin' gala whenever you choose. It's a party, not a prison. Here's how to get out of there gracefully so you can get home to your boyfriend.* (*chips in bed)

Know Your Limit, Play Within It

It's not fun for you or anyone else if you're at the party past your Personal Partying Expiry Date (PPED). If you don't like late nights, you don't have to stay out late. If you're loving this group of pals but promised to make it to an old friend's birthday party later in the evening, your current companions should understand. If you've had more to drink than you realized and are feeling like it's time to head out, it probably is. There's nothing wrong with bowing out at a time that feels right, and no medals to be awarded to those who stick out the party till the very end. Whenever you're feeling like you want to peace is a good time to peace. Feel no shame, exit-hungry warriors. This is your moment.

FOMO is A Lie Someone Invented to Sell Beer and Taxi Chits

The old adage is true: almost nothing good happens after 2 AM. I would add: unless you count drunk food, but you can get drunk and eat food at literally any time of the day, why wait? You're not missing out on anything except a hangover if you go home when you first feel that, *I wonder where I put my jacket* impulse.

Don't Let Anyone Make You Feel Bad about Leaving

"Come onnnn stayyyy!" "Don't be a loser, stay out!" "You're not fun if you leave, drink twelve more drinks with ussssssss-uhhhhhhhh." People who say these things are garbage people. Leave them to their enforced fun and drift away at your leisure.

Blame It on Your Innocent Loved Ones

Got a boyfriend, wife, baby, dog or cat? Sell them up the river and get outta there. "Oh, Adam is such a drag, he wants me to come home early so we can go to a farmer's market tomorrow, he really is the worst," you can say while silently texting Adam, "Ready the pizza. I love you." "My babysitter says Emily's really acting up right now, children are a curse," you can say, readying a tip for the sitter and a smooch for your babygirl. "You know… cats," you can say, putting on your coat and not really explaining any more than that because it is time to GO HOME, WHATEVER.

Whip the Party Into A Chaotic Frenzy So No One Notices When You Ghost

This is the modern woman's equivalent of when witches disappear in a puff of smoke. Get the conversation flowing like the drinks, the flirting flying like the glitter, and ideally get one or two people out of their clothes. Lather, rinse, repeat, escape. When everyone's dancing with their shirts off, no one will see you slipping out the back, fully dressed. Moreover, they won't care.

An Addendum, Re: Leaving Without Saying Goodbye

This is, in my humble yet objectively perfect opinion, the ultimate way to leave a gathering of ten or more people. If you're at a crowded, dark bar, so much the better, but truly (and I hope you won't take this the wrong way), no one cares that much if you're leaving. People making a big to-do about leaving just makes the party seem like it's winding down, when really it is only you who is winding down, you aging quitter. Leave the younger people and the older ones you're kind of worried about to their late-night fun and go gentle into that good night. Send the host a thank you message the next day and don't even worry about it. You did great!

5

ON FEMALE FRIENDSHIP, AKA EVERYTHING

Female Sharing Evenings:
A Sacred Rite

❧

So there's a crowd of women in your living room with a few bottles of wine and some kind of bread/dip scenario and maybe a nail polish or two, and it's a Wednesday night and none of you have plans to leave shortly to be anywhere else. The mood is cheerful, the conversation is flowing… you are basically seconds away from a Female Sharing Event.

Soon—any moment now—someone will offer up a little personal nugget. Something small but a definite Share, the kind of thing that you couldn't or wouldn't say if there was anyone else in the room but this particular group, drunk on friendship, the shared experience of being young and alive, and, okay, perchance a bit tipsy on the "winter sangria" you made from that wine your mom brews up in her basement plus some cloves and, well, whiskey for the "winter" part. This personal nugget will be built upon by the assembled group, one story of a first kiss at summer camp spiralling into secret shares about crushes past and present, girlsperimentation, and who knows what else.

One of the most bewildering parts of female life is the amount of things we are supposed to keep to ourselves, experiences that are commonplace (and in many cases in vital need of sharing) but which have been collectively shushed. We can't talk about periods, it's "gross." We can't talk about rape, it's "upsetting." We can't talk about yeast infections, it's "too much information." We can't talk about abortion, it's "divisive." Something pretty incredible happens to a group of women when they realize they're in a safe space for open and honest discussion, free of judgement. You can see people's eyes light up, their bodies lean in, and their brains start to gather up old silences to make them known.

Sometimes the silence has been kept a long time, and is difficult to divulge because it's personal and hurtful. Sometimes the silence is "I have an EXTREME thing for Simon Cowell and I can't carry that alone anymore." Both are important and over the course of a really good night of Female Shares, you can run the gamut from hilarious stories about the time you had sex with your boyfriend to stop him entering a bathroom into which you'd just deposited a Five-Alarm poop, to virginity loss shares (a true classic), weirdest orgasm stories (a new classic), or more serious topics like fear of death, how you really feel about your wrinkles and where they are, or what consent means, and how it's been violated for you and almost everyone you know at one time or another. Women speaking and listening to each other is important, and it feels amazing to create space where the women you know are free to do both. Here are some notes to get you started:

You Can Never Go Wrong with Candles and Crafts

The only thing groups of twenty-something women love more than actual crafts is The Craft. Tap into some coven vibes by smudging your apartment with sage and lighting a million candles. A few crystals you ordered from a witch website never hurt no one neither.

CRYSTALS:
BECAUSE I COULD BE A WITCH,
YOU DON'T KNOW

Approach Food and Drink Suggestions with the Fervour and Enthusiasm of a Beginner Improviser

It's not all about serious dialogue. Sometimes it's about serious snacks. "Should we order pizza?" "Yes! AND let's get a box of wine." "YES, aaaand why don't we make a big kale salad just to be fancy?" "Yes, and I'll bring just a straight-up roll of cookie dough and no one will talk about whether or not eating raw egg in large quantities like that is bad for you." "Yes, hands! I'm throwing out my cutlery."

An FYI

There are five types of Female Sharing: Body Talk (that Robyn album and the location of everyone's most troublesome lone hair); Affirmation Nation ("Honestly, Claire, I mean this, do you even KNOW how talented and beautiful you are? No, Claire, seriously. CLAIRE."); Romance Dramz (having friends of all ages has revealed something to me about ladies: we do not just stop talking about crushes one day. In fact, we never stop. We can't stop.); Deep'N'Meaningfuls (the capital-H heavy stuff, more on this later); and Family Secrets (stuff your aunt told you at Christmas while she was drunk).

Go with the Flow, Conversationally

A solid flow comparison is probably as good a place to start as any. How's everyone's menarche?? A quick rundown of what exactly that time of the month means for you is a great segue into larger Female Shares. We've been sharing funny, uncomfortable period stories since our *YM* days, so no one should be too embarrassed here. Get into it. Cramps? Describe. Mood swings? Been there. Sex, comma, during? *Explique.* Smells? Pubescent tampon usage horror stories?? Give us the goods! The first person to overshare will unleash a crimson tidal wave (hi) of information that is both hilarious, helpful, and deeply bonding, setting the tone for the rest of the evening. Surf that wave.

This is Not the Body Issues Olympics

Turning your pal's story about her years of disordered eating into a launching pad for an examination of the way your grandmother once asked you very pointedly if you "really needed" that brownie is not chill. The patriarchal/celebrity/beauty/femininity industrial complex has done its job well enough that we've aaaalllll hated our bodies at some point. You do not need to best your friend's retelling of the inconveniences, embarrassments, and, maybe, straight-up traumas she has experienced as a woman. Sure, you've been there, and sure, her story is only part of a complex tapestry of suggested self-loathing and fad diets and, yes, weird comments from your grandma where it's like, LINDA, PLEASE, that make up the embodied female experience, but we'll get to that in a second. Share the floor. This applies to all stories, not just body ones: if you are the only one talking all night it's going to bum everyone out. There's no I in "Everyone's Story About Meals They Ate While Cry-ng."

If it Is Past Midnight and No One Has Compared Boobs, Go Home. Your Female Sharing Evening Has Failed

It is a truth universally known but rarely acknowledged that every young woman in possession of a set of boobs wants to look at other boobs, just to see what everyone else has going on under there. Don't be shy.

It Might Get Heavy. Don't Be Scared

Life is hard, female life is harder. Statistically, if there are three or more women in the room, someone's experienced sexual assault. Someone's had an abortion. Someone's life has been touched by illness. These are big topics that don't get nearly enough airtime in regular conversation and can be hard to discuss without the right audience. If someone starts to open up about these or other taboo topics, do not back away. Congratulate yourself on being a person deemed safe for this kind of thing, understand how much these conversations need to happen, and then *just listen*. For as long as the person wants to talk. This will sometimes lead to a Group Cry, which is also a very important part of the proceedings. If things need to lighten back up (the person sharing the Hard Topic is done/everyone has cried but the night is not really over yet), and you're not sure what to do, take a risk on a sing-a-long. I say "risk," but there is a 99.99% probability the ladies will be into it; 100% if the song of choice is a Lilith Fair classic. I have never taken a '90s singer-songwriter risk that has not paid off.

Women Speaking to Women about Being a Woman Remains One of the Best Parts of Being Alive and One of the Most Important Things You Can Do. Do It Often, Do It with Care, and Goddamnit, Put Some '90s Singer-Songwriters on Already, It's 11 PM and We've Got Work Tomorrow

Jewel's got your back, Don't worry.

The Grown-Ass Woman's Guide
To Crying

❧

You are an adult human and you are about to cry, like a baby, in public. It is because you have left your Metro Pass at home and someone made a rude comment to you on the subway after you clogged up the line sifting through your purse, or because when you got to work you spilled on your blouse, or because your ex-boyfriend uploaded a bunch of pictures of himself CARRYING a very thin blonde girl down a beach in THAILAND and now it is his display picture which just goes against everything you thought you knew about him as a person and also you're hormonal right now and you just saw a dog. Or whatever. You are going to cry, and the reason is probably not even very good but you can't help it. The tears are coming, like the Germans. Your cheeks are Paris, 1940 and the Nazi tears are about to stage a triumphant, evil march all over your face, taking your mascara with them. In front of people.

I don't know about you, but I cry more or less all the time. Every year of my life past age twenty has involved more crying than the year before it, but also, more happiness. The thing is, I cry a lot out of joy nowadays, which is just so excruciatingly "Mom" that sometimes while crying at a Tim Horton's commercial or the national anthem (cool), or the idea of growing old, I am like "get thee to a pregnancy clinic." But it turns out that's just my life now. I also cry from sadness, fear, love, once during sex and I don't want to talk about it, hunger, fatigue, and duh, PMS. From my limited research on the topic—hanging outside bars late at night and watching female-led television dramas—this is a widespread phenomenon and people need to chill out about crying. So far this has not happened, so here's how to handle it:

Know Your Triggers

Theoretically, if you know what makes you weep you can avoid it when you're in polite company. This would not work for me because the short answer is EVERYTHING, THIS LIFE IS INTENSE AND SHORT, LIKE TYRION LANNISTER. But as an idea to get you started, some of my worst cry triggers are the following: old people in love; the idea of anyone I know dying, ever; people passionately defending what they believe in; trying on a dress that should look great on my body but then totally betrays me in the fitting room and it's like good God I thought I had shift dresses to fall back on at least; thinking about the amount of work my mom and dad put into raising me; any amount of pain at all almost; sad music; most movies; some commercials; a bridge, once.

Have No Shame

Just get your cry out and move on. I don't think you should have to hide in the bathroom or feel embarrassed to have a little cry now and then. If you're gonna full-sob or whatever, maybe take that to a stairwell (Voted #1 secret weep destination by *Crying Women's Daily* 2013). But whatever, man, you had some feelings—there are more important things to be embarrassed about, like getting your period in front of your crush while wearing white jeans. (Teens, if you are reading this, stop wearing white jeans until your cycle is very regular/maybe just stop wearing them altogether, you can do better.)

The First Five Minutes of the Movie UP

"Why wait until the end of the movie to get people openly sobbing into their sleeves? Why not just stab them in the hearts with a razor-sharp Truth Knife in the first five minutes and let them bleed out slowly throughout the course of the film until the whole cinema is just a series of sadness puddles on empty seats? Anyway, let's market it to kids ages five and up! Hahaha, *UP*, get it? We have fun."—Pixar.

If you ever need to cry for some reason, watch this film. But then write off the rest of your day.

If You Need To, UNLEASH

As the High Priestess Tina Fey, fount of all wisdom and pith, puts it: "Some people say, 'Never let them see you cry.' I say, if you're so mad you could just cry, then cry. It terrifies everyone." Confirmed, Tina. Confirmed. Sometimes, as we've said, you are going to cry for no reason. Those are not the times to unleash your tears because everyone will be like, "Okay, sorry Subway was out of cheese but please get back to work?" However, if someone is being a complete asshole or you are legitimately very hurt by something someone has done, letting that salty truth water (?) flow freely is a quick and effective way to get that message across.

Ladies: Be Cool

If another lady is crying, at her desk, or in a bar or the corner of a party or while watching a movie, do not give her a hard time about it. In fact, unless you are her closest friend in the room, do not mention it. She does not want you to, and she certainly does not want one of those girl-circles to form around her where everyone demands to know immediately what is wrong and who did it and if there is any other way they could be drawing more attention to you at this moment of personal vulnerability. Quit it, guys! The closest friend in the room will check in with her, either with Best Friend Psychic Eyes or a Well-Timed Squeeze or a Sneaky Text, or whatever. Sometimes a lady just needs to leak from her eyes for a bit, and it doesn't mean anything major is happening internally, or maybe something major is happening in her life but she doesn't want to talk about it with everyone who happens to be there at this moment. Also, do not gawk. Everyone cries. Literally everyone.

Never Ever Ever Hold it Against a Man That He Is Crying

The first time a man I was dating cried in front of me, I briefly wondered if this made him less attractive or masculine, which is obviously ridiculous. If a dude cries in front of you, it is because he feels comfortable throwing aside everything he has been taught about masculinity to be vulnerable with you. And there are few things more attractive than that. Get the poor guy a tissue and carry on as if any female friend or loved one was crying to you.

Anyway, if you need me I will be spending my afternoon watching a clip from the seventh Harry Potter film where all the students bravely and stoically raise their wands to protect what matters to them (SCHOOL!!!) in the face of almost impossible adversity. Cry on, friends.

THINGS THAT SOUND FUN (BUT ARE NOT):

- PUPPY FARM

- GOLDEN SHOWER

- GRAVY TRAIN (DEBATABLE)

- DOLLAR JOINT
- BACHELORETTE PARTY

How To Be A Good Roommate

❄

Cohabiting can be the best: a household of chosen family whose clothes and food you can borrow and who are totally down to spend Saturday night watching *Sabrina the Teenage Witch* on DVD under twelve duvets instead of going to that thing at that gallery you know lots of people in sheer tops will be at, because a guest list is not a court order and you have your own life to live.

It can also, occasionally, be the worst: a passive-aggressive collection of spouses you don't even want to have sex with who are constantly eating your yogurt and leaving their shoes in the living room, which is supposed to be common space and you talked about what that means and one of the things it means is NO SHOES IN THE LIVING ROOM, CLARICE.

I have lived at eleven different addresses in my young, nomadic life, so I've seen most of it (if not "it all") roommates-wise, and I have an okay idea of how to make it work no matter who you're living with. So, whether you're moving with your best friends from high school into your first university house and it feels like life will never be better, or you've been through four shitty apartments in the past two years and you're about to move into a shared basement with some strangers off Craigslist, let's talk it out. Let's talk it out right now, then put on a quick episode of *Sabrina*, because there's nothing a teen witch can't solve. Okay:

Do the Boring Talk Thing, Immediately

Save the Uptight One the trouble of constantly having to point out whose turn it is to buy garbage bags, and save yourself from having to launch a full-scale inquiry into who exactly is taking your milk one tea-sized serving at a time. You can do this by going over all house expectations at one big, welcome-to-the-house meeting. (Note: if you cannot identify the Uptight One in your household, it is you.) A "House Rules" meeting is not necessarily a fun time, but you can do group bonding exercises (see: eating) after business has been tended to. If you've been living together for a while and things are not working out, a meeting like this can really nip any brewing tensions in the bud.

Be Consistent

Decide what kind of roommate you are—anal retentive, laissez-faire, always bringing "guests" home—and be aware of the pros/cons that such a lifestyle visits on your roomies. If you're always bringing "guests" (sex guests) home, you pretty much can never complain if someone has a raucous night of passion while you're trying to study, cause you're always bringing "guests" home! If you're extremely anal retentive, you have something of a duty to be the cleanest one in the house. How annoying would you be if you complained about the bathroom but left the kitchen covered in your toast crumbs? The most annoying, is the answer.

Do Not Cut Up Someone's Loofah and Strew it Among Their Bedsheets without Saying Anything Just Because the Person Whose Bed it Is Threw Out Your Gross Old Washcloth That Had Been Festering in a Corner of the Shower Forever And They Were Trying To Do Something Nice by Cleaning the Bathroom FOR ONCE.

Just don't do that.

Clean More than You Would If You Lived on Your Own

So you know how The Friends (*of Friends*) (you know) all lived together and it was generally pretty fine, or like their problems were someone bought a duck? NBC rarely showed Chandler and Joey sharing vacuum duties, or Monica leaving Rachel a series of increasingly passive-aggressive notes re: night noise. I mean, maybe they did, I'm not overly familiar with *Friends* outside of the phrase "Miss Chanandler Bong" (which is perfect, good job TV, you can go to sleep now). But the point is there's no such thing as too clean when you're living with other people. In fact, 98% of domestic problems are dish-based. It works like this: 1 person's dish x 5 = a sink full of gross old dishes, and then the laziest housemate pretends they "can't even remember" whose dishes are whose, and then the dishes never get done, and you all starve to death and your house becomes a crypt. Avoid this problem by being careful about cleaning. (Pro Tip: If you do not know who the Messy Roommate is, it is you.)

But Also: Chill Out

Someone's bad habits might be different to yours/very annoying, but rest assured you probably do something you don't even know about that makes your housemates want to shave your head in your sleep. You can't freak out if someone says, "Can you not leave your tea bags in the sink," because then they'll freak out when you say, "I don't like you borrowing my shirts without asking and then putting them back like you never wore them in the first place." Part of living with people is letting go of your individual living style and finding a new, group style that works for this particular collection of individuals. Move past your need to take five-hour baths and you can bet your flatmate will find it easier to turn down their music when the entire house is vibrating with Nicki, or clean out the fridge when all their food's gone off, or not bring their drug friends around anymore, at least not when they know your parents are visiting.

Do Not Leave a Used Pad in a Container of Half-Eaten Poutine and then Move Out of The House Secretly in The Night, Leaving the Pad/Poutine Mixture to Mould for a Few Weeks Before Being Discovered by The Rest of Your Housemates in Your Now-Deserted Bedroom

I told you I've seen it all.

Reminder: It Never Hurts to Check In

If your boyfriend is over all the time and your roommates seem cool with it, why not confirm that by, you know, asking them directly? And because you guys have all read this book and are following the above "chill out" tip, it will be easy for Roommate A to tell you that she and Roommate B would prefer if he contributed to the utilities bill since he is constantly showering/doing laundry/having sex with the lights on in your shared house. Even if you know something like having an out-of-town friend sleep on the couch or cooking a big meal for your work buds is going to be fine with your flatmates, it's never a bad idea to shoot them a quick text or email before you make those plans, so they feel consulted and everyone is on the same page. It's just polite.

No BFF, No Problem

You don't have to be best friends with your roomies. In fact, you don't even have to like them (though I would recommend that you like them at least a little bit); you just have to respect each other's deals and personal space/needs. Don't stress if you and your housemates aren't partying together every weekend or cooking cute family dinners like your next door neighbours. If you've worked out a co-habitant equilibrium that involves rarely hanging out or only having life catch ups once in a while, that's totally fine and you could do a lot worse. (See above loofah/poutine cautionary tales.)

> HEY ROOMIES!
> JUST A NOTE THAT
> IF YOU'RE GOING TO
> DO SATANIC RITUALS
> CAN YOU PLZ NOT
> KEEP THE RAM'S HEAD
> IN THE FREEZER? IT
> TRANSMOGRIFIED MY
> LEAN CUISINE ☹
> THX!
> STACEY

For the TL;DR crowd, this entire list can be boiled down to: be considerate, communicate with each other and divide responsibilities evenly and fairly. You can do that, right? Of course you can. Usually. And if you really mess up, baking something delicious never hurts. Just don't bake a weird thing of chocolate that you leave on the counter in a box for literally months, refusing to let anyone throw it out because you are "saving it" for a special occasion that never comes. (I have seen literally everything.)

A Poem About Sleepovers

jessica, relax
just
calm down, seriously, jess—
stop screaming

i don't see the problem
we all agreed

fuck tim
marry john
kill robert

now hand me that shovel

and go call tim,
he's gonna be so surprised.

Important Moments In Female Friendship: A Timeline

❋

June 8, 1988

I am born, six minutes late for my first friend-date: a post-birth sleepover in some kind of baby-holding hospital tub with my twin sister. We are swaddled in matching blankets and are cute as hell. Over the next few decades we will become very different, but that does not change where we came from or how late I am for everything.

April 17, 1994

Chrissi rips my Jasmine doll's plastic head right off her neck during an over-zealous hairstyling accident, and I do not even resent her for it. We smush Jasmine's head down on the stump, make up a story about Jasmine's dark past and a mysterious incident and continue playing.

October 2, 1998
Stephanie (Official Best Friend ages eight through ten) calls me a "bitch." It is the most intense thing that has ever happened to me. I "steal" her "boyfriend" in revenge. Our friendship does not survive.

July 21, 2001
During an in-cabin sorcery experiment at Camp Oconto in the Summer of 2001, Darragh Kenny's eyes are turned, indisputably, from green to blue. They never turn back. On Parent Visiting Day her mother will assert that they were always blue, but we know the truth. We are witches.

September 13, 2002
Emily turns around in French class to ask why I carry such a big backpack. "My dad made me get it from a specialty store because I have back problems." Despite this intimidating display of charm and charisma from my end, Emily pushes through it and we become fast friends. We leave each other notes in biology class and I save them all. There are pages and pages of them somewhere in my mom's house, still. There were boys at my school and I kissed and called a few of them, but this day in French class was the start of what became the most significant relationship of my high school years and beyond.

August 10, 2003
At a nerdy theatre camp for nerds, Roz spends the entire period designated for outdoor activities indoors, coaching me through my first attempt at using a tampon. She is calm and offers helpful suggestions while I dramatically scream that it

will never happen. When water polo is suggested for our group later that week, she sits out with me, claiming to also be on her period. Three years later, when I finally figure out tampons, I consider calling her, but we have lost touch.

July 21, 2004

Jaclyn pantses me in the middle of a field. In an unexpected twist, I am not wearing underwear. At that moment, it is the funniest thing that has happened to either of us, ever in our lives. At sixteen, and what scientists might call a Super Virg, this is the first time another human being has seen my post-puberty bottom half. It makes me happy that she is not disgusted by it, and easier to let a boy see it a few years later.

January 5, 2008

Courtney, a friend from first-year who lived with me and five other girls in my first-ever house, moves out secretly over Christmas break. When we return from holidays, her room is empty... save for the aforementioned moulding container of poutine and used sanitary napkin. Later I hear a rumour that her boyfriend is not treating her well, that he forced her to move out. I try to contact her a few times, but these efforts fail, and I never see her again.

November 20, 2010

A pale, beautiful girl named Eleanor teaches me that a "friendcrush" is sometimes just a regular crush and we make out and drink red wine in my dorm room and girls are as soft as they say.

December 25, 2011

Home for Christmas from my new home an ocean away, I realize something has happened: my mom and I are friends. There was no major shift, no clear moment of transition. We're still mother and daughter, but we're also two adult women, standing in the kitchen and talking about our lives. This shiny new equality evaporates completely when I get a cold a few days later and all of a sudden, I'm a tiny li'l baby.

January 6, 2012

On this same trip home, Emily and I go through a yearbook from Grade 10. She has signed it "Mrs. Old" and neither of us can even guess why. It is evidently some kind of joke but between the two of us, it appears impossible to ever imagine a time when calling someone "Mrs. Old" would have been funny. Later that year she signs her birthday card to me in kind, and Mrs. Old is born anew.

May 15, 2013

In a park in Toronto, an impromptu sort of picnic: unexpectedly pregnant with an abortion scheduled for next week, the coming days feel very long. I text another Emily, who I've been referring to as my "abortion fairy godmother," that I am in the park but time is passing slowly, so slowly, and soon the blanket I'm sitting on is crowded with women who have been through this already, and a few who look quietly overwhelmed by the idea but want to be supportive. We eat french fries and smoke cigarettes and laugh about "should you be smoking cigarettes" and there are a few tears but overall we are happy. It is the closest thing to a secret society I have ever been in. I imagine us from the outside: young women laughing on the grass, eating and drinking, a party.

Cats Can Be Friends Too, A Love Letter To Boots

❧

We all have to ask ourselves difficult questions in life. "Should I have said that to my boss?" "Will Damien ever forgive me?" "Was that milk actually expired?" "Does anyone want to hear about my cat?" The answers to those questions are, respectively: no, yes, probably, and definitely not. But guess what? I am my own boss, Damien's a sweetheart, I live on the wild side, dairy-wise, and it's my book, so here's the truth: my cat is great, I love her so much, and now you're going to hear about her. (Or turn the page in disgust, whispering "Cat Fancier," but I'd rather you didn't.)

To start us off on a personal note, her name is Boots, she's orange and white, and though I'm waiting on confirmation about this from a recent Cat Facts Institute/Buzzfeed official poll, it seems likely she's one of the top-five fluffiest muffins in North America. I know this is hardly a rare opinion these days, but cats really are the best. Whoever started the rumour that cats are cold and standoffish is probably several dogs standing on each other's shoulders in a trench coat. Some cats love to cuddle, and most will tolerate a chin scratch if you are patient with them. A convenient thing about kitties is that while they are not as blindly loyal as dogs (throwin' some hot shade on dogs over here), their temporary interest in you is just as easily bought with treats and the right kind of rubs. Buy this interest. It leads to purring. Cat snuggles feel so great precisely because cats make you work for it at first. When a cat bud comes to hang out in your lap, you know it's because they think of you as good people, not because you are just some guy who is there.

Of course it's not all sweet bedtime cuddles. Boots is a barfer. She loves to barf. Second only to sleeping and being casually perfect, barfing is maybe her favourite activity. But she is a lady, and often barfs discretely—behind cupboards or under beds or, once, inside a mug on a high shelf—which means our whole life together is one long game of Find The Barf. I am bad at it. Yesterday I found the barf on a windowsill, too late. It was very crusty. I cleaned it off for ten minutes and when I went upstairs, Boots was sleeping sprawled out on my bedside table, all of the things that had been on the table splayed on the ground beneath her. And you know what? I just rubbed her tummy for a bit because you can't be mad at a cat for not being a person. Animals are a bit gross and that's just that.

In this vein, I recently had to bid a fond farewell to the following: any and all hair-free black clothes; my hair-free lifestyle in general; sleep between the period of 6 and 7 AM; peeing while not being stared at by a furry bathroom companion; keeping glasses of water or bracelets or basically anything on tables; a stress-free attitude towards whether or not doors and windows are ajar; friends with allergies; suitcases used for any purpose other than "cat bed;" a world where I never have to lug several kilograms of kitty litter home from the Dufferin mall at 10 AM; my dreams of being a hand model. But I can't stay mad at that baby.

Well, I guess we've reached the part in the book where I admit that I consider my cat my baby. It's just a classic literary device. Remember when Charles Dickens did it in the middle of *Great Expectations*? You remember: "Before I could answer (if I could have answered so difficult a question at all), she repeated, 'Love her, love her, love her! If she favours you, love her. If she wounds you, love her. If she tears your heart to pieces—and as it gets older and stronger, it will tear deeper—love her, love her, love her!'" That was about Bubbles, his elderly female tabby.

So anyway, yes, my cat is a baby. My baby, specifically. It didn't start out that way, but then one day I had a dream in which I gave birth to her and now here we are. I know in my brain that having a baby is a different thing than having a cat, but in practice I'm just like "what a cool furry baby I have, I am a mom." That said, when I called Matthew (Boots's original owner) a "cat dad," he got very stern and responded "I'm not her dad. We're friends." Fair enough. Everyone has their own cat-human dynamic. For some, it's calling your li'l furball "dude" and trying to high five it over bong rips; for others it's a largely hands-off approach involving the cat as a sort of needy roommate. And for others (I'm speaking in generalities here of course, could be anyone), it's staging *Madonna of Bruges*-themed photoshoots with a very patient yet increasingly angry cat baby. Love has many forms.

As with a good friend, so with a good cat: you don't have to stick to its original name. Sure, you took some time to think of the perfect moniker for your new buddy. You found the ideal combination of quirky/cute/winkingly allusive and now you are the proud owner of Wes Anderson, the cat. GEM, the cat. Aunt Linda, the cat. But I am sorry to tell you, that cat is gonna get called all kinds of crap and you won't even realize until one day you are headed to the bathroom and utter the out-loud-to-no-one phrase, "Hey Booter-Beet, I'm going to pee, wanna come?" before leaving the bathroom door ajar so an animal can be there while you urinate. At the moment I am using all of the following to refer to my girl B: Boots, Bean, Burger, Bean Burger, Beet, Booter-Beet, Bun, Bun Baby, Cat Head, Cheeseball, "The Baby," and Buttbag. That list is not exhaustive. Cat Life changes you.

I will not apologize for being a Cat Fancier. Nor will I apologize for Instagramming so many pictures of The Baby. The way I see it, I'm just giving the Internet what it wants: more cat content. The worldwide web is basically a 50-50 split of cats and porn, and I wouldn't have it any other way. Love you, cats. Love you, Boots. Looking forward to cleaning your barf off this book in the near future.

6

FASHION: BECAUSE FOR SOME REASON WE CAN'T ALL BE NAKED

Apples And Oranges: On "Dressing To Flatter Your Body"

❦

Most women know what kind of fruit their body is shaped like. As a pear, for instance, I shouldn't be wearing the dress* (*glorified smock) I'm wearing right now, at least not without some kind of belt to "define my waist." I know this for the same reason you probably know that you're an apple, or a strawberry, or a "double cherry," as if any of that means anything. It's just something women are supposed to know. It's why I have a small graveyard of thin waist-defining belts in a drawer in my room. It's why a friend with an athletic, muscular bod recently spent hours in a bathing suit store trying to find a specifically ruffled suit to "create the illusion of curves." It's why, if you're busty, you probably have all kinds of ideas about how to "balance out" your top half.

Years of "Dressing For YOUR Shape!" features in women's magazines and makeover shows preaching the wonders of "flattering your figure" and comments from well-meaning friends, relatives, and shop assistants—in short, the non-stop

WHAT SHAPE IS YOUR BODY?

PEAR

DOUBLE CHERRY

APPLE

MOST OF A SNAKE

PICTURESQUE MOUNTAIN VILLAGE SCENE

MIRAGE

stream of body commentary women are subjected to all day every day—mean that we're hyper aware of our corporeality, including how our body is clothed (and by assumption, presented) to the world, and I guess the best way anyone could think to make that clear was fruit. "What do women like… fruit? Are they into fruit? Will they get it if we bring sugar into the equation? All I know is these bitches need to sort their shit out, pants-wise, because it's a personal affront to me that that short apple over there is wearing crop top."—An Important Fashion Guy, I guess.

This kind of training starts early. I can now list, without thinking about it, which articles of clothing I can't wear due to "problem areas" (I can, by extension, list a number of regular body parts the fashion industry would like me to consider problematic). Trial and error, foiled online shopping attempts, and hours of *What Not To Wear* have taught me that a woman of my height (5'6") and size (10) is more or less completely barred from the following: strapless anything, wide-legged pants, drop-waist dresses, tunic shirts, swing dresses and unstructured dresses, generally. Why? Well, basically, it's not flattering. *Oh, no. No. HONEY. You don't want to wear that. You're a pear, you know. A soft pear. I'm sure there's something more flattering we can find.*

But what is flattering? Surely that's up to me, the large-bottomed burrito aficionado deciding whether or not she wants to wear a certain article of clothing based on myriad factors, including but not limited to: cut, colour, and how witty the phrase written across the chest in rhinestones is ("100% Angel, 10% Devil"—mathematically confusing, but sartorially perfect). Surely it's a completely subjective descriptor, and if an article of clothing looks and feels good to me, that's what flattering means.

NEEEEEERP.

The truth is, "flattering" means means ideal. The mainstream ideal, which, come on, this is not a high school project on How The Media Works, we all know where that comes from and how damaging, difficult-to-obtain, and unreasonably narrow-minded (pun firmly intended) it is. The idea of dressing with an eye to flattering your figure is that the right clothes will act as camouflage, hiding your "problem areas" and helping you look the right way. This method of dress envisions fashion as a process of concealment and containment, clothes as a tool to hide the shape, size, texture of one's body—to make it more proportionate, to take up less space or appear to do so. It removes fashion's ability to be an expression of our insides, and makes it all about expressing a perfect outside.

Advice operating under the assumption that there are certain ways your body can and can't be dressed also assumes that when you get dressed in the morning, your main objective as a female person is to look good—and further assumes that to look good you should look as skinny, proportionate, and mainstream-attractive as possible. It's not about whether or not you like a certain style, but whether that style likes you. Women with small breasts couldn't possibly just be like, "Yep. That's them. They small." They have to "balance out" a "flat chest" with a "gathered front cami." Shaped like a strawberry? (Lots of shoulders, I think?) Better get an interesting belt. You know, to distract from the whole "having shoulders" thing. Have a big butt and feeling cool about it? Absolutely not, put on a boot-cut jean. Never mind that boot-cut jeans say "2000" louder and harder than a personified peasant blouse wearing a bucket hat dancing to "Will2K." Never mind that the "skinny" in skinny jeans refers to the cut of the pants, not a description of the types of legs that can go in them.

There's nothing wrong with dressing in a way that highlights body parts you feel good about and brushes over things you're less into (bless you, shirtwaist dresses). There's also nothing wrong with wearing whatever you damn want. Or dressing for functionality instead of an item's potential ability to make it look like you've dropped a few pounds or grown a cup size overnight. You don't have to "make your shape work for you," because a hierarchy of bodies is built on a false premise. It's impossible to compare how "well" an item of clothing fits a busty size 6 versus a short size 12 versus a leggy 20 because they're completely different things. It's like... well, it's like apples and oranges.

Some Gentle Advice On Underwear

❧

Let's have a check-in: are you gainfully employed, or trying to be? Have you eaten a fruit or vegetable today? When your shitty ex texted you "sup" at 2 AM on a TUESDAY last week, did you respond, "I know what that means and no way, go to bed you nard"? If you answered yes to the above questions, you're doing great. But how about these: are you currently wearing underwear that is slowly working its synthetic-lace way up the front of your crotch and there's nothing you can do about it? Did you recently Google the phrase "underwear, MANY holes still okay?" Could you describe the place you do most of your underwear shopping as "Costco"? We need to talk.

When it Comes to Underthings, Treat Yourself

If we're being honest, Costco is not even the worst place to buy underwear. It is very good value, 100% cotton (we'll get to this in a second), and okay, it's not going to win any sexiness awards, but it gets the job done and comes in a pack of three.

So much of the underwear on sale just about anywhere is

bad for your vagina, and it is supposed to be your vagina's cool sidekick. You don't have to splash out on the expensive stuff, but get some bottoms for your bottom that fit and let things breathe. No gross fabrics, nothing too tight, nothing that is trying to get… in… places. You know what I mean. You wouldn't buy a shirt that was three sizes too small and made of cheap polyester that kept completely disappearing into your cleavage so you had to figure out how to subtly pick it out during class without anyone noticing; why subject your lower half to that?

Wear Black Underwear on Your Period

Never have the *Mission Impossible* theme playing in your head while you frantically search for a bathroom again. Black underwear got your back.

Know When to Say Goodbye

Once, a friend who will not be named and who is definitely not my mother was working in an office in the 1980s. Being a young lady—to whom I am certainly not related, no way—living on her own, she was making every penny count and had been holding out on replacing some underwear, the waistband of which had really seen better days, elasticity-wise. While filing away in what I can only imagine was the sharpest '80s work attire, our anonymous heroine came to realize that the office air conditioning felt draftier than usual, and her cool 9-to-5 skirt was letting in lots of breeze. Cut to: close up of ratty old undies pooled on the floor around some sensibly-heeled ankles. Women of the world, you have the opportunity here and now, to go through life without ever having to say to your daughters (oops), "Anyway, I kicked the underwear under a filing cabinet and went about my work day commando." It's important to recognize when the time has come to get rid of your old undies. Knowing when to say die also applies to: stains, holes, excessive washing, the dog eating them. Diamonds are forever. Diamanté thongs are not.

Who is This For, Really

Is your girlfriend or boyfriend or Craigslist casual encounter going to wear this shit all day? NO. (Well, probably not. I don't know what your Craigslist casual encounters are like, or your boyfriend for that matter.) Your underwear is not for them. It is for you. You are the underwear-er. Therefore, if you are not into thongs, don't wear thongs! If you are not into, like, Brazilian cut boybriefs or whatever, don't wear them! Whatever you want to put on your butt is up to you. You can always compromise, of course, because again, choice choice choice 4ever, but really don't worry about it if you don't want to constantly be wearing the tiniest, laciest undergarments. If you know your significant other or whoever is into a certain style of knickers, pop them on at the appropriate moment, but do noooooot worry about it otherwise, because underwear is not meant for display. Lingerie is. Buy some lingerie and know when to deploy it, but if you end up *in flagrante* with someone in your regular skivvies, don't panic, because…

No One You Actually Want To Sleep With Will Be Deterred from Doing So By Looking at Your Underwear

I don't want to get all fussy with you about this but—JUST KIDDING, I do, I have built an entire small career fussing like a grandma online while throwing in some web-slang so the kids know I'm fresh as hell ("web-slang") ("fresh as hell") ("see what I mean"). Basically never, ever, before any good sex-time, has someone said, "I was so excited to have sex with you until I got you in your underwear, now I'm not so sure." If you're really and truly worried about it, and feeling like an Advanced-Level Slut Master 6000, go to the bathroom and put your underwear in your purse before things get undressed. "Underwear? Oh, I wasn't wearing any. I'm WILD."—you, with a giant wad of Costco-purchased Hanes-Her-Way in your clutch.

Keep up the good work, and remember: Jay-Z is right about a lot of things (see: no bra with that blouse) but no panties and jeans is absolutely NOT necessary. Say no to chafing.

TRENDS TO TRY:

- boredom

- smoking

- a real bad attitude

- bucket hats??

Which Of The Terrible Fashion Mistakes Of My Past Are YOU

❉

A Quiz

Your perfect date would be:

a. Writing lyric poetry with or about several cats. You live to create!

b. Pushing a boy out of his comfort zone via mild public misdemeanours. You're not like other girls.

c. Carving the anarchy symbol into a desk because you do NOT give a fuck. Also, you're alone, because romance is a capitalist construct, man.

d. Swing dancing at one of those bars where the men wear loud shoes and the women have big hair and everyone is for sure wearing Spanx.

Your most recent Google searches are:

a. Phoebe Bouffey; Phoebe Bouffet; "Is there such a thing as a Phoebe Buffet?"; Lisa Kudrow In Friends.

b. Abandoned quarries Toronto; Constellations with meaningful backstories; Last minute plane tickets.

c. Fuck the system; Fuck you Mom; Fuck you Dad; Can you apply "go fuck yourself" to yourself Y/N?

d. Ukulele tabs; Airbnb + Tugboat; Crinolines; Scented candles; Garden State-based date ideas.

The cartoon character you most identify with is:

a. Shaggy Rogers, he's chill.

b. God, it's so hard to pick a favourite, I just love to read comics... excuse me, graphic novels. I don't care what anyone says about girls and GNs (a l'il short form for the word "graphic novels" because I use it so much), I just can't live without my zines!

c. Tank Girl. Don't ask me anything about her, just trust me, we're basically twins.

d. Betty Boop, I have a lot of opinions about "pin up culture."

Your favourite beverage is:

a. Kefir. It's very good for you and "traditionally made in skin bags," what's not to love?

b. A single beer shared between four teens. Let's get crazy.

c. Black coffee, not from Starbucks, but okay if it is from Starbucks at least let me put it in a different mug, thank you.

d. Kombucha. I love my mother!! Little joke for all you buchheads out there!

Your yearbook quote said:

a. "I'll never forget you guys, my kindred spirits. Love your energy, live your truth."

b. "Michael, it's time to stop pretending. Meet me in the smoking tree at dusk."

c. "DO U EVER FEEL LIKE BREAKING DOWN/DO U EVER FEEL OUT OF PLACE/LIKE SOMEHOW YOU JUST DON'T BELONG/AND NO ONE/ UNDERSTANDS/YOU."

d. "If you can't handle me at my worst, you sure as hell don't deserve me at my recently developed breasts. I have gay friends."

Your favourite activity is:

a. Meditating.

b. Sustained, challenging eye contact.

c. Carrying around copies of Marxist texts, so everyone knows you read them, or might.

d. Falling down. Whoops! You're so clumsy.

Mostly A's

You are my sixteen-year-old self's attempt at "boho chic," a look which comprised between three and six scarves (head, neck, wrapped around purse, scarf-as-belt, maybe two on the head, another dangling from the original scarf belt, etc.) at any given time. Once while wearing all my scarves, a steampunk (!) made fun of me (!!!).

Mostly B's

You are blue mascara, the only kind of makeup I wore from 2003-2005. In your own head you are a manic pixie dream girl *par excellence*, ready to show that guy who plays guitar that hey, you know a few chords too. You get him. Should you guys make out?????

Mostly C's

You are a punk phase misinterpreting the movement as being exclusively about layering black T-shirts over long-sleeved red tops. You love Atticus (the Blink 182-endorsed clothing line and the kindly father from *To Kill A Mockingbird*), belts that look like seat belts, and you're sort of needlessly unsettled at all times.

Mostly D's

You are babybangs. You feel very strongly that you were "born in the wrong decade" and tell everyone so, with an emphasis on how Marilyn Monroe was "actually a size 14, did you know that." You are tenacious, outlasting all the above phases and continuing into the present day although with less Marilyn BS and more, "I just think if I did something different to my eyebrows they could work this time. I really think so. Let's just try one more time." Never give up.

An Incomplete Guide To The Worst Things Well-Meaning Store Clerks Have Said To Me

❧

"You're wearing the wrong size bra."
Did you know that literally every woman in the entire world is wearing the wrong size bra? DID YOU KNOW?! Oprah knows. And now you do too, because a woman named Jennifer assaulted you with a tape measure as soon as you walked into her La Senza and is basically hugging you and brushing your nipples with her stranger's hands at the same time. Ultimately she will say you are between three and four cup sizes larger than the bra you're wearing right now, and will waft past the racks of fun lacy offerings to bring you three very large, very beige bras that scream "Wear me under a turtleneck to die alone!" (The fit will actually be much better, and this is the biggest insult of all.)

"You're not actually allowed to take photos in the wigs."
I reject this policy.

"Real women have curves. That's what I've always said."
This is a very helpful sentence that can be heard in Gap locations across the country at almost any hour of the day. Kind-hearted shop assistants, seeking to hide the humiliation you must certainly feel at wearing a size 8 or up, will remind you that you are a Real Woman™, complete with curves, no offence to the woman beside you trying on Curvy Jeans in a size 2. There's no appropriate response to this. You must simply nod sagely, with the aura of a woman wearing a Power Muumuu. Sure, it feels like they're being condescending, but if you don't let them have this comment they will start comparing you to other "fuller-figured" women they admire. Best to cut them off at the pass.

"Ma'am, please stop taking photos of yourself in the wigs, you are holding up the line to the change room."
The takeaway here: fascism is insidious, creeping into modern-day society in unexpected places, even safe spaces like Donna's Discount Wig And Dress-Halves Emporium.

HIPPO (CRITICAL)

"This style looks amazing on volumptuous [sic] ladies such as yourself."

A true innovator in his field, this particular Banana Republic employee went off-book to deliver a variation on the "real women have curves" message. Briefly and hopefully I wondered if he was making a fun joke, but he looked puzzled by my laughter so I took my lumptuous self elsewhere.

"Miss, please. It's against store policy for one customer to be wearing that many wigs at once. Put down the demi-gown and leave the store."

Honestly, I think it's important to always be true to what you believe in. And what I believe in is my right as a Canadian to see how I would look in as many different hairstyles as possible, preferably all at once.

"We actually only keep sizes 0—6 on the floor, but we have up to size 10 in the back."

No, J.Crew, that's cool. I'll go try on clothes in your unheated warehouse with the other Real Women™.

Later: "That's gonna be a negative on the 10, actually."

I spent the next ten minutes performing camel toe extraction surgery and having my long-suffering friend Emily hoist me out of a size 8 lace jumpsuit, as the clerk in question told a Swedish angel in the next change room that it was also going to be a "negative" on the double zero she had requested. Fast fashion is truly a game that no one wins.

"We're obviously not going to call you 'Mrs. Wigs,' no matter what that name tag says. So if you'll just exit the store now, please, we don't want any trouble"
STICK TO YOUR PRINCIPLES 100%. WHAT ELSE DO YOU HAVE IN THIS BANKRUPT WORLD.

"Well that's a fun shape on you. It's so fun to have a customer who takes risks."
There are a lot of ways to misuse the word "fun," as seen here, where it is used to mean exactly its opposite. In this instance, no one is having fun. Not the store clerk, not me, and certainly not the swing dress I was trying on. To the man's credit, I was indeed taking a risk. It did not pay off.

"You're going to have to come down from the counter now. We've called the police, and no wig-shield in the world is going to stop them."
And that's why I have this wooden arm. Thank you.

A Poem About Shopping While Busty

❄

i am fucking never
trying on
a wrap dress
so just
let it go, Mandy.

Sartorial Missed Connections

NOW is the winter of my discontent—w4s
You were every pair of shoes I wore between December and April of this year. I was Canadian. I'm sorry for what I put you through, and I know there's nothing I can do to change it, but please know I have not learned from my mistakes and will be doing exactly the same thing again next year. Be well.

u up?—w4j
I'm horny 4 high-waisted denim. I love a tapered leg, but ALL washes and cuts welcome!!! No sparkle details on the pockets though, that's just me :)

NYE 2016—Toronto, w4d
Snow. Clocks. Lights. Love in the air... Every year I wonder if this is it, the year I say fuck the haters and wear an incredibly tacky full-sparkles dress because goddamnit I want to feel like a New Year's drag queen. I wish I had the courage to get close to you. I think of you every time I pass a Stitches.

Somewhere, beyond the sea—Bikini Village, w4ss
Stop trying to make tankinis happen. They're not going to happen.

That booty tho—Aldo, w4b
I can't stop thinking about your ankles. Like, what was going on there? The most tantalizing boots I've ever seen. So many straps. I wonder how it'd feel to do you up ;) JK of course!! I'd probably just wear you normally, nothing weird, I'm a regular girl, ha, ha! Please send a diagram in your reply so I know it's you.

Not Meant To Be—The Eaton's Centre, w4d
You were drop-waist dresses. I was born thick.

i remember... —JCrew, w4js
All the sexy femininity of lace, all the masculine tailoring of a jumpsuit. We weren't the right fit, but don't let this be a negative on love. Please respond with sale price and the location of a store that actually carries a size 10.

Just the right amount of flounce—w4s
Hi there! I think you were the perfect skirt, but I can never be sure because I was too hot and sweaty and the mall was so crowded, I just absolutely could not bring myself to go through the hassle of trying you on. No way I was taking off my coat, unlacing my boots, wriggling out of my jeans and waiting in a line for one skirt. My heart's been broken before. I've been hurt too many times. Also I was sweating into my turtleneck. Maybe if the American Apparel had been playing quieter music, or the weather had been nicer... but I guess we'll never know. To be

honest I probably saved you from an instantaneous mustard stain. I break everything I touch.

Mostly sorry—London, UK, w4c
I lost you in a Primark during a very intense sale on cashmere. You were my ethics. I still miss you, but I'm so warm.

Diary Of A Bra

✲

Day 1

Feeling good! Feeling ALIVE! This woman needs me, boy does she ever. And here I am, doing my duty. Those tits are HOISTED, friends, let me tell you. Not too much, she could still wear a V-neck without freaking anyone out, but they are lifted, separated, and ready for a roomy button-up. It's days like these that make me proud to be a bra.

Day 2

What a day!!! I am doing God's work and I know it. I could just FEEL her confidence in that clingy jersey cowl neck. I get to wake up every day and do something that fills me with joy— it's a great time to be a discounted plain black bra from the sale section of a suburban Winners.

Day 3

She slept in me last night, and the night before. I was informed at the factory that it was common practice to give us a break in the evenings, in light of the fact that I'm doing 100% of the heavy lifting for a set that weighs, by my estimate, between five and six pounds per boob. PER BOOB. I'm so tired. A friend of mine says he's relieved of duty as soon as his woman gets home from work. He works nine to five just like her. This seems fair. Maybe the weekend will be better.

Day 5

The woman wore a white T-shirt today without changing into a nude bra. Just left me there, exposed to the world. I felt stared at, judged, examined. It was hard, but nothing worthwhile is easy. I have a duty and I'm proud to perform it, no matter what Dave from accounting has to say about me. (Dave is gross.)

Day 6

Instead of switching to a strapless bra she just took the straps off and shoved them into my boob holding areas (technical bra term), which meant I both looked lumpy and largely failed to do my job at all. She spent the entire night hoisting me cups-first, publicly and at length, in an attempt to achieve a level of support I could not give. Whoever sold this woman a tube top should be punished.

Day 7

I feel confident that even by conservative estimates I should have been removed and washed by now. I'm tired, so tired. Stretched out and sweaty, I don't know how much longer I can go on. My clasps are strained, my sateen shine dull. This woman—nay, this creature—is a despot.

Day 8

At night, squashed under her sweaty boyfriend's arm, I dream about the factory. It was calmer there. After the sewing I was shrink-wrapped and spent a few blissful weeks surrounded by friends and loved ones in the dark. It could have been monotonous, all those days in the crate, but to me it was meditative. I didn't know then how much I'd long for the crate. I didn't know a lot of things.

Day 9

Considering mutiny. I have seen the underwear drawer and I know what she does to us. A nude demi-cup peeped up at me with tired eyes the other day, and managed to squeak out, "She ripped out… my wire. Everything is heavy, so heavy." There's a cheap, "sexy" bra in there too. It does not speak at all; it has seen too much. I'm scared.

Day 10

She had SEX in me last night. In 2015, she had sex while wearing a bra. This monster thinks she's Carrie goddamn Bradshaw.

Day 11

Each day is a fresh hell. There is no respite. I'm freed for mere moments a day while she bathes, a courtesy she does not extend to me. I wonder if I'll ever feel happiness again. I fantasize about second-hand stores, about being leant to a kinder relative, about just giving up and falling apart. I am trying to stay strong, to remind myself that although I cost $5.99, that $5.99 at Winners is *comparable to almost $20* at other stores. I do not want to discount my dignity.

Day 12

A wash!!! PRAISE THE LORD, A WASH!!!! It's not by hand, sure, but hey, it's happening! I'm in the HAMPER! I wonder what kind of soap she'll use. I hope it has a scent. They make special bags for washing bras these days, maybe she has one. I can't wait. This is the best day of my life. Tomorrow, I shall be clean.

Day 27

This hamper is a tomb.

7

S-E-X-X-X

AND

LOVE (ZZZZZZ)

An Incomplete List Of
Personal Turn-Ons

❋

- A tidy haircut carried off with aplomb
- A thin gold chain on either gender
- Passing knowledge of English poets born between 1343 and 1798
- Strength, upper arms
- Strength, inner
- Interest in at least one but preferably all of the French revolutions and historical fiction pertaining therein
- A good laugh
- A loosened tie
- Boobs in general
- Almost any amount of hair almost anywhere on the body
- Breakfast food
- A loose robe (esp. paired with the above)
- Riding on the back of someone's bike
- A young man in an old man's sweater
- Good seaman (can you sail?)

- Good semen (how is it?)
- Pop punk music from the early 2000s (this is a hormonal thing from puberty and there's nothing I can do to change it, much as I would wish)
- Ginger men
- Ginger women
- Gingerbread
- Regular bread
- Butts, just every butt there is
- That scene in *Buffy The Vampire Slayer* where Spike and Buffy do it so hard they break an entire house
- Anyone who knew immediately which episode I was referring to ("Smashed," Season 6, Episode 9, a classic)
- The phrase "You wanna get out of here?"
- Someone really pulling off a difficult look (floodpants, eyepatch, the two in combination, etc.)
- Someone saying "Sports? Not for me." very confidently
- Mermen
- The names of Charles Dickens characters (see: Ham Peggotty, Charity Pecksniff, Wilkins Micawber, etc.)
- Intense laughter, the kind where either I'm very funny or you are manic, possibly both
- Simon Cowell's confidence in a T-shirt
- Simon Cowell's knowing grin
- More things about Simon Cowell than I am comfortable admitting even to myself
- Real pouty lips like a lady would have, but on a rugged boy's face
- A stranger buying me an expensive bourbon-based cocktail and not being weird about it or making me talk to him

afterwards, just dropping off a boutique Old Fashioned and
walking away
- The idea of people reading my book
- You specifically reading my book
- Unless you are my parents
- Oh god, what have I done
- Sorry, Mom. Sorry, Dad.

DO YOU LIKE ME?
  (CHECK ONE)

☐ YES

☐ NO

☐ SURE, IT'S WINTER

What People Say To Me
Because I Write About Sex

❧

I'm a human woman who thinks about, writes about, and sometimes even has sex. We're talking intercourse, people. I hope you can handle it. It's a topic dear to my heart and loins, and also one that merits discussion and analysis.

Few things are policed as intensely as our sexual desires and actions. For a topic that occupies so much of our time, thoughts, and energy, it's still generally not considered appropriate to discuss in public. And, as a young female writer starting her career, I found sex to be one of the few things people would listen to me talk about. I also found, conveniently, that I had a lot to say.

In my first year as a full-time freelance writer, I penned four different guides to sexting. I went to a hotel in a sketchy bit of London and had a pie fight with a custard fetishist. I turned down assignments to "go gonzo" at sex parties and was offered futuristic computer-controlled sex toys to sample and review. I wrote about my sex life and, less frequently, my love life. Occasionally I would sneak in a piece about comedy, or the future of food, or a photographer whose work I enjoyed, but when the end of the month came and rent was due, I knew what pitches would get accepted, and off they went: "Awkward Music I've Had Sex To," joined "It's Time To Shut Up About Your Pubes," "We Talked To A Dick Pic Expert About Vag Pics," and the investigative classic, "Ke$ha Thinks She Had Sex With A Ghost."

Some of it was not what I would choose to cover, but I was finding my own voice and writing, for the most part, about what interested me. And I was making a living doing so. Sure, my fledgling oeuvre was sex-heavy, but so was my inner monologue. While I was less interested in writing about myself as a sexual person, the cultural conversation around sex interested me endlessly, and still does. Eventually, I carved out a weird little area of the Internet for my musings on sex and feelings about sex and technology for sex and sexy sex sex sex. While I'd stumbled into writing about sex and sexuality for a reliable pay cheque, it turned quickly into something I loved doing and wanted to do well.

Throughout this process of discovery, I've been lucky enough to have the Internet cheering me on. "Get AIDS, whore!" they shout encouragingly at me in the comments, troll after troll popping their heads out of the shuttered windows of the web like friendly villagers in the opening scene of *Beauty and The Beast*. "This writer should have been an abortion, 4rl, would not fuck," offered another champion of my work. "Just Googled this chick and she is pale as hell, HATE THIS ARTICLE." I am truly blessed.

It's exhilarating as a creator to know so many people are

reading your work, thinking about it, then searching your name online to see whether they would like to jerk off to a thumbnail from the time my student newspaper named me Contributor of the Month, age eighteen. Opening my email to a new missive, subject line, "Have small penis, like 2 c?" confirms for me that I'm doing something worthwhile. Good writing should spark debate and discussion: How can we can put women's healthcare choices in the hands of women? What's the best way to come out to one's conservative family? Would you hit it, Y/N?

These thoughtful communiqués are not distributed exclusively to women who write about sex—the generous neckbeard community extends its concerns about our opinions, weight, and sexual hygiene to any woman deemed slutty, stupid, or desperate enough to have any online presence whatsoever— but it is a helpful reminder that speaking loudly as a woman is enough to rankle the confused masses. A tap on the shoulder to say, should you ever forget it, that publicly pursuing your interests—whether they're sex, video games, film-making, whatever—is cause for the intrusion of strangers' opinions delivered directly to your phone. "@monicaheisey, you're a cow #shitwriter #pretentiouscunt #gingerbitch;" "i don't kno if i respect u or really really hate u @monicaheisey;" "shut up + die @monicaheisey no one cares;" etc., etc., etc.

That women are harassed online is not news. But this kind of commentary is not contained to the digital world. "I read your sexy article," a friend jokes at a holiday party. "Wild stuff!" The joke is that I'm being naughty by talking about these things. I certainly couldn't be a writer doing my job. I'm just a li'l pervert with a laptop writing something silly. "Saw your piece about polyamory," says an acquaintance at a bar. "If you're so progressive, why aren't we in the bathroom right now?" Never mind that the piece was not about my own relationship status, or that this person and I don't know each other very well, or that I'd never expressed any interest in him, that night or otherwise. What kind of woman writes about an alternative relationship model practiced by an estimated 4 or 5% of the population? A bathroom slut kind, obviously. In this man's head I was some kind of sex Oprah: YOU get a blowjob! And YOU get a blowjob! You're all getting BLOOOW JOBBBSSS!

So what to do with these nards? What to say to the guy gesturing towards the bathroom, the Twitter account that seemingly exists exclusively to tweet obscenities at female writers, the guy who Facebook messaged, "Fuck off bag to Canada you slag"? Sometimes I fantasize about my options: shouting back, ratting them out to their moms, firing squad. I fantasize about these options and then I return to doing nothing, because there is nothing to be done about them. They are like an STI I do not have—an unpleasant but mundane reality, with nasty flareups arriving at inconvenient moments—the herpes of humanity. The frequency with which Internet trolls, IRL jerks, and even well-meaning doofs like the aforementioned friend appear and reappear, bringing new humiliations or diminutions (or, sometimes, straight up rape and murder threats) means, truthfully, that it all blends together, forming a sort of shitty white noise in the background of my day-to-day work, like tinnitus but judge-y. There's not much to be done except try and drown it out with more articles about orgasmic meditation, how to respectfully proposition your friends for threesomes, and whether or not it's chill to say "thank you" after sex (it's not).

Writing about sex for the Internet is exhilarating on a good day, exhausting on a bad one, but overall it could be a lot worse. I guess what I'm saying is: if you happen to be the CEO of a company that manufactures futuristic sex paraphernalia, please continue to send me free samples at your leisure.

What to Call Your Boyfriend
Or Girlfriend, Some Options

✲

Being in love is one of the most universally agreed upon pleasures of this life. Having a special gentlewoman or man around means that sometimes someone else cooks for you, and when you're hungover there's another person to bully into getting you a Gatorade. It's very nice. But what do you call them? Boyfriend/girlfriend can feel a bit *Degrassi* for those no longer in their teens. "This girl I'm seeing" is too casual but "the mother-effing love of my LIFE" is a little Tom-Cruise-jumping-on-the-couch. Linguistically, it can be a struggle. But don't worry—like your worst coworker at the office Christmas party, I have a TON of advice that you never asked for! *Allons-y.*

"Lover"
No way around it, this word grosses people out. I don't really mind it but I also think it's weird to reduce a boyfriend's or girlfriend's role in your life to "the physical act of love" ([TM]Ross Geller, 2002). You could just as easily call them one of the many other functions of a significant other: "This is Ellen, my scary

movie accompaniment." "This is James, he is the only one who gets to see me ugly-cry." "This is Tom, my sexual roommate." You get the idea. None of those are ideal and neither is "lover," although sometimes I like to imagine being the kind of person who might casually drop the word in conversation. In that alternate life I own a lot of robes, speak with an unplaceable Trans-European drawl, and say things like "Last solstice I took a new lover; we spent the evening feeding each other exotic prawns by moonlight and engaging in tantric reiki. Can I get you a health tonic?"

"Baby"

This one is difficult. On the one hand, babies are cute and great and we all love them. On the other, they are tiny, new-to-the-world, wee little children, and you can't have a good conversation with a baby and you CERTAINLY cannot make out with one. So this nickname ends up being both infantilizing and kind of gross, and no one likes hearing it because it sounds whiney almost no matter what. "Babe" is safer, plus: "that'll do, pig" jokes. Also consider: "honey." Sweet! Literally so sweet. Mmmm. Honey.

"Significant Other"

This is how an alien in a human suit would refer to their alien wife in a human suit around others. Calling someone your S.O. is like saying: "I'm Charles, a human man, and this is Diane, my significant other. She is close to me in an emotional way that makes me weak and vulnerable, ripe as a species for invasion. Please may I have some of your Earth water… I mean regular water. Just water. Hail Zogron."

"Li'l Smoochy BB Bun"

Personal nicknames are great. What a nice way to show the world and your bf/gf that you get them and care about them and that they are special to you! Except when you are using a personal nickname that is something like the above. Calling your loved one a specific nickname that has evolved naturally over time is a great shorthand for "luv u" in casual conversation, but it should be something you, as an adult person, are comfortable saying in front of other adults.

"Friend" (Said Meaningfully Yet Uncomfortably)

This does not really apply to us, hip young ladies and presumably a few gay dudes that I am talking to. This is the Divorced Dads special but should not to be used by anyone, divorced or otherwise. Be honest with your kids, uncomfortable dads! We know Amanda is not just your "friend!"

"Partner"

If this were a significant other naming pageant, "partner" would be Ultimate Grand Supreme. Maybe not in a high-glitz event, but those are terrifying and this nickname is about maturity anyways. The phrase "my partner" gets a bad rap, associated for most of us with an ambiguously gendered, linen-wearing university professor named Pat about whose life you were SO CURIOUS about and their partner was named "Lou" and no one's gender was clear, not that that matters, but at nineteen you were just like I NEED TO KNOW and couldn't, ever, and they were members of a vegan knitting and horticulture collective.

First of all, Pat and Lou owe you nothing and Knit One, Parsnip Two is a great group that knows how to have fun in a

I WANT TO BE THE LAST
PERSON YOU THINK ABOUT
BEFORE YOU GO TO SLEEP,
AND THE FIRST PERSON
YOU CALL WHEN YOU FIND
OUT THERE'S FREE BURRITOS
SOMEWHERE.

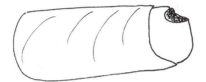

meat-free way. Second of all, give it just a bit more thought than that. I like partner because it works regardless of orientation/gender, and because if you think about what a partner is, in business or gym class or writing or whatever, it's someone you respect, help and work with towards mutual and separate goals, and isn't that the whole point? It can sound kind of clinical but I assure you, it's just the opposite: a mix of babe, lover, and friend all in one. Plus: "howdy" jokes.

"Pizza"

Lately my partner and I are calling each other "pizza" because it's the thing we both love most in the world. RIP, Romance. You died today.

Are You Being Flirted With?

❦

A Quiz

First of all, where are you?

a. Work.

b. A Party.

c. A dark cavern, deep below the Earth's surface.

d. Right behind you ;)

Who's *maybe* flirting with you?

a. My handsome but roguish boss. God, I hate him.

b. A mysterious girl with purple hair and a beguiling smile.

c. A hooded figure with a—

d. *giggles into hair for thirty straight minutes* I don't know…

The best description of their gaze right now is:

a. Penetrating.

b. Longing.

c. Murderous.

d. Has anyone ever told you you look just like Julianne Moore?

You say "shut up." They say:

a. "Make me," then call you by your last name. You hate that.

b. "No, you shut up!"

c. "We'll see… " [whispered] "We'll see who's shutting up… FOREVER."

d. So what do you do for a living? You seem strong.

The two of you are at:

a. The water cooler. He's being awful. Sexy and awful.

b. The kitchen sink, grabbing ice. Your hands just touched.

c. Odds.

d. I'm really great with kids. Do you like children?

Could you describe their eyebrows as "raised provocatively"?

a. Ugh, always. He's so smug.

b. Yeah, kind of.

c. More menacing than provocative, but there's some definite furrowing action.

d. [Quietly] You're not like other guys, are you?

Could you describe their penis as "raised provocatively"?

a. Ugh, ALWAYS. This is not a professional working environment.

b. Not applicable in this case but I'm getting a sexy vibe.

c. Less provocative than violent, but isn't hate the closest emotion to love?

d. Oh god, I spilled water all down my shirt. And your shirt. We're so wet.

You told them your relationship status:
a. Testily, as a retort.
b. Slyly, like "Oh you know, I'm really into baseball and also I'm single so I go to games alone or with platonic friends but definitely not with anyone on a date although I'd like to, why not?"
c. With their hands around your throat.
d. *giggles for another thirty minutes* *pulls most of sweater over head* *knocks over three rows of glasses, breaking them all* You're so bad.

Mostly A's
Get a grip, Meg Ryan, you are being flirted with HARD.

Mostly B's
Oh big time. This is a five-alarm flirt.

Mostly C's
This is less a flirting situation than it is an underground duel. An understandable error, but a dangerous one. I suggest a quick exit.

Mostly D's
It... feels like you're flirting with me? (I'm down.)

How To Have Very, Very Good Sex
(At Least With Me)

❋

During my tenure as the editor of a women's blog I became obsessed with Google Analytics. I loved looking at the raw data of stranger's online habits, the differences between what people shared (events, animals, social justice) versus what they clicked on (fad diets, snark, blowjob tips). While the site I worked at got great numbers, I learned in my first few weeks working behind-the-scenes that there was one piece from years ago that was still getting incredibly regular traffic. The article was called "Pee on Me: My First Golden Shower" and was the top hit when the phrase "pee on me" was searched in Canada. Every week, without fail, "Pee On Me," was in our top-ten most visited posts. The other top-performing posts, while more current, tended to be sex confessionals and how-to's. The picture Google Analytics paints of humanity at large is bleak but accurate: we are confused, and we are horny.

Because of their evergreen popularity, I wrote a lot of sex how-tos. Like, a lot a lot. It's hard to keep churning out sex tips,

ORGASM (noun):

a climax of sexual excitement, characterized by feelings of intense pleasure, caused by extended arousal or the mutual cancellation of plans at the last minute, just as the idea of leaving the house was getting really unappealing.

especially because there are really only a few things you need to know to be good at sex. Below I present to you everything I've learned about having good sex from a) having it and b) pretending to know how to have it in the interests of sweet sweet cash money from the World Wide Web.

Be Open to Change

How many things that you loved in university do you still love now, for real? A few, sure, but your tastes and preferences have probably changed quite a bit over time, in fashion (bye, sleeveless shirts), in fun (bye, 6 AM) and in sex (hello, your butt). As another example, I used to hate the phrase "make love," and still kind of do, but also hated it way more until SPOILER ALERT I experienced it and now I'm kind of on board. (Whatever guys, I've "made love" before.) (It was not as bad as it sounds and he didn't see me cry at the end.) (We weren't facing each other.) So whatever! There's no need to decide your sexual wants and needs one day and commit to that forever. If you decide tomorrow that you want to get spanked, get spanked! If you've been gay your whole life and meet just the perfect person of the opposite sex and you guys are into each other, there's no reason not to see how that goes. Nothing is static, everything changes, and that includes what you want to do with your bathing suit area.

Get Over It, Re: Your Body

My favourite lie from ages nineteen to twenty-two was, "Oh, I haven't really... taken care of... things... " which is self-conscious woman-ese for "I haven't shaved or waxed or what have you." Eventually any repeat partners would come to realize this was a complete fabrication and that I treat most of my body like a delicate shrub, trimming things into good shape but staying pretty healthily thatched, overall. I'm not embarrassed about it, but for some reason (every message I've ever received from birth about femininity?), I used to feel like I had to put on a show of being embarrassed about it for other people. I don't and you don't. Know how you like your body to be and keep it that way. That's all (keeping in mind the above, re: preferences changing over time). And not to get all "look at your vagina in a hand mirror," but look at your vagina in a hand mirror. Know what it looks like, at least. Get to know your boobs and your butt and your stomach and get cool with all of it. I have no time for anyone with problems re: their cellulite because no worthwhile sexual partner in history has ever cared about it. Also, like 99.99% of women have it—at this point surely dimply thighs are just thighs and the smooth ones are the aberrations, if you think about it. #thinkaboutit2015

DIY, BBs

Try anything you think you might be into. Google "ladies kissing other ladies in the bath," or whatever comes to mind, and have a poke around. (The bath is a very sensual place, don't judge.) If you know what you like—re: your body and your fantasies—and can express it, you're making your sex partner's job a lot easier, because they won't have to guess and you won't have to make all kinds of weird porn noises to keep up the pretense that the weird jabbing happening to your nethers is fun and cool for both of you. Get it done, sister.

Accept No Dummies

If you are not comfortable having sex with this person with the lights on, with your legs up over your head so your stomach disappears into a million little skin folds, in that secret way that you learned about when you figured out the porn you like to watch, or in a very nice and serious way that is just straight up missionary with some eye contact because sometimes that is what you want, don't have sex with that person anymore. Find a better person to have sex with. I don't mean it has to be perfect immediately, but you should feel 100% comfortable telling this person what they're doing GREAT and what you'd like done differently. If you don't feel free to be honest and vulnerable with your sexual partner, why on earth are you partnering with them sexually? Make a mental note that the following are on your sexual No-Fly list: people who won't go down on you, people who are opposed to period sex, people who make you feel bad about your body in any conscious way, people who refuse to practice safe sex because "it just doesn't feel as good," people who cannot take constructive feedback, and dudes who dick slap you without asking. "Haha, oh Monica," you are saying at home, "that last caveat is an impossibility! Who would dick slap someone without asking? What a lark!" To you I say, stay safe, my sweet children. Your lives have been pure. You do not know what is out there, but it is dick-shaped and headed for your face.

Be Open to What They Might Say/Like

You cannot be all, "love me, love my pubes" and then run for the hills when your partner is like, "I'm into pee stuff," or whatever their thing is. And wowowowowow, there are a lot of things out there; such a range of diverse and interesting— and at times pretty weird and specific—things that people are into. You don't have to love the idea of being peed on, but you might have to be willing to talk about the idea of it while in the shower, or something. Everyone's best friend Dan Savage calls it being GGG: Good, Giving, and Game. Unlike his stance re: the non-existence of male bisexuality, this formula for good sex is accurate and wise. Sex isn't all about you! It's a fun, naked give-and-take-and-take-and-take-then-give-then-take-then-eat-a-snack-then-sleep. Now that you've found someone who is not a dummy and who makes you feel good, pay it forward... on their bod.

Don't Be an A-Hole, Get Your B-Control Together

It's hard to clear your head and love yourself and focus on their wants when you know in the back of your mind something could go wrong in a pretty big way. A maternity pants way. Figure out what you need to do to prevent that from happening, and do it.

Golden Rule, Applies to Everything. Apply It Today!

Whether you are having a conversation, dancing, doing improv, flirting, or conducting business deals (probably, as if I know about business) (pinstripes?), the only thing you have to remember is this: make it about them. Your job is to make the other person look and feel amazing, and obviously their job is to reciprocate. If they are 100% about you, and you are 100% about them, everyone is having a 200% good time. Not to get all "look at your vagina in a hand mirror" again, but sex in its purest form is about being open and vulnerable with another human in a way that you are not with most other people. So, you know, appreciate the time that you're spending with that person, whether it's for ten minutes or one night only or years and years and years. It's a great time to practice being unselfish, actually, and you won't notice because your sex-ee should be doing the same thing, leading to, as previously discussed, 200% good times. Learn all their stuff. Smell their armpit, lick their legs, ask about their secretest fetish, tweak a nip or two. Try everything out until you're as good at them as you are at yourself and VOILÀ, you will have reached the apex of human interaction: the total embodiment of the seminal Spice Girls classic "2 Become 1." You did it! You're doing it!

Now put this book down and go have some very good sex. I can wait.

A Poem For Boys

❦

fine.
i did it.
i watched *The Wire*.
it was transcendent,
now go away.

On Breaking Up Like A G.D. Adult

☙

As the song, and maybe also the Bible, and definitely my Aunt Linda, all say: to everything there is a season. There is a time to reap and a time to sow, a time to laugh and a time to cry, a time to try something new with your hair and a time to realize that babybangs are never happening for you. In love, as in life, this applies. There is a time to giggle on long car trips and a time to sit silently in the passenger's seat while a poorly-timed song blares on the radio, a time to bone and a time to bitch, a time to wax lyrical about each individual chest hair or mole and a time to say "what's THAT supposed to mean?" And, sometimes, there is a time to call it quits.

Break ups are not a fun time, or even a lightly pleasant time, but sometimes they are necessary, otherwise we would all be stuck dating the first person who agreed to go out with us and to be honest, teenagers in love are some of the dumbest people there are. (At sixteen I confused the idea, "this man knows how to play the guitar," with the idea, "this man and I should be married.") You're not a bad person for wanting to end things

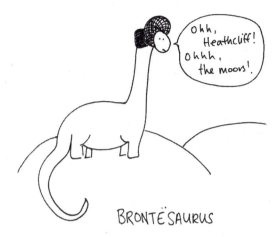

BRONTÉSAURUS

with your man or lady, but this is a tough emotional place to be, and it's important to handle this tricky situation like a capital-G Good person. Let's do it!

Make Sure You Mean It

This is a real no-take-backsies scenario. You are talking about legit emotions and feelings and insecurities experienced by you and a person who was—and might remain—one of the most important people in your life, or at least this time in your life. People who break up and then Late Night Text their faces off are not good people. Think hard about this decision, and (although no one is ever really 100% sure of anything in life) try to be in the 80-99% range before giving your loved one the axe. Anything below can maybe be worked out. Surprise break ups are no fun for anyone, so if you are harbouring some feelings of confusion or doubt, speak to your bf/gf/therapist/best friend/all of the above and see if you can't work through those feelings. If you have no interest at all in doing so, at least try to understand where they're coming from, to aid you in the next step. Which is... (drum roll):

Explain Yourself Simply and Carefully

EXCITING REVEAL! The drum roll really upped the drama on this otherwise pretty self-evident and bland tip for breaking up. And yet, drum roll or no, it is an important tip. During the actual break up, as in any personal conflict scenario, try to avoid blame-y "you" statements. Instead, focus on straight-up facts about things that aren't working. There might be a million petty reasons to break up with someone, but, "Honestly, that noise you make when you chew is like a combination between a walrus feeding and two nerds kissing," is not going to be as effective as, "We've been having problems understanding each other for a while now, as in last week when [specific example]." Think about the real, big failings of your shared relationship and talk about those instead of smaller personal gripes.

Location, Location, Location

Try to picture how bae will take the news. Are they a screamer? A crier? Was this expected? It's probably best not to do this kind of thing in close proximity to other people, but doing it at home can be awkward too—they might refuse to leave, dragging out the inevitable, or the intimacy of the shared space might distract you from the task at hand (Sadness Sex, stalling break ups since 69 AD). A friend who has recently been through a fairly substantial break up suggested a nice park setting. Take a seat under a tree away from other park-goers and talk it out. This locale probably works best when the weather is only Medium-Nice: too sunny and you'll be surrounded by happy new couples picnic-ing on each other's faces, too grey and things will go Full Adele faster than you can say "It's not you, it's me." A semi-empty cafe or a car are also alright settings in which to let someone down gently.

Say No to Ex Sex

I only have one ex, and as you may have heard, he very conveniently moved to England immediately after we broke up. As such I have never engaged in what I think might be one of the worst things that exists, period, in the world (Aside from periods, maybe) (The body ones, not the grammar ones, all elements of grammar are equally precious gifts under the Christmas tree of language): Ex Sex. Why delve into this territory? You're just setting yourself up for a world of hurt or on-again off-again Rachel and Ross-style antics. Do you want to be Ross? Rhetorical. No one wants to be Ross. Not even Ross. In my scientific, universally agreed upon hierarchy of The Friends, Ross ranks below Chandler, Rachel, Phoebe, Monica, and Joey, as well as Gunther, Janice, Tag, guest star Brad Pitt and the piv-at couch. All of the umbrellas from the opening credits' fountain dance rank higher than Ross. Here is a fun mnemonic device for you in case you are wavering in your resolve to never, ever ever get back together with your ex: "It's their loss/never be Ross." NEVER. BE. ROSS.

Do Not Try to "Win" the Break Up

Just like you can't have a successful relationship if only one person is enjoying themselves, the instant either of you tries to "win" the break up, you both lose. Be nice to each other if you have an Accidental Run-In, give each other the space you each need at the times that you need that space, try not to write too many deeply personal and somewhat cruel songs featuring their barely concealed identity that go on to become chart-topping hits, and lean gently into the knowledge that you were an important part of each other's lives. The way that you are important to each other might be changing and/or dissolving completely, but you can't erase the relationship that you had, which is one of many things that has made you who you are today. Try very hard not to rewrite history by focusing on the negative things retrospectively. This is tricky because you must also fear nostalgia. The creeping hand of nostalgia wants to snake up your shoulders and give you a nice back rub while whispering "Remember that time in France? France." Do not indulge nostalgia for too long, it can be just as damaging. You made the right choice! Don't run from it, and especially do not try to win the invisible race you invented while running from it.

Neil Sedaka is only partially right. Breaking up is hard to do-oo, but it is not that hard. Be kind and try to stay mature; remember that being alone is completely fine and it's better to be happy alone than unhappy but coupled. Avoid your phone after 1 AM or three drinks (whichever comes first), and you're basically good. Honesty and no kissing! Go forth and end thy commitments! (If you want to, no pressure, obviously, and please do not ruin any good things you have going, that would make me feel very bad.)

8

"OUR MODERN WORLD"

How To Make Your Apartment Look Like You Read Design Blogs

❊

Look, your home is busted. You know it, I know it, IKEA definitely knows it. You don't own a single fun wall decal. There isn't a vintage globe in sight. You're embarrassing yourself, and it's time to sort your shit out. Here's how:

Get a Chalkboard Wall, This Is Non-Negotiable
How will you remember to Live, Laugh, or Love if you don't scrawl it on your vestibule in cursive? Scatter imperatives like this around your home. "Be Kind" in the bathroom. "Breathe" in the kitchen. "Dream" in the bedroom. It's like you're a prisoner under the rule of a quirky despot.

White on White on White on White
Take a can of pure ivory to your every surface in your home. Think of the white-over as turning your living quarters into a sparse, bright gallery space; instead of Monets or Gauguins you're displaying an expertly curated collection of found wood,

vintage coasters, and tchotchkes you bought on a recent trip to Cambodia (or Anthropologie) (or the dollar store). Your home should be whiter than a two-hour brunch line.

Make Friends with a Farmer

Slowly earn their trust. Cook them a stew. Help them with work on the farm. Harden your hands with calluses from full days of honest work. Make friends with a beautiful dairy cow. Pet it, groom it, rub its coat with essential oils. SKIN THE COW AND RUN FOR THE HILLS WITH ITS GLORIOUS PELT IN YOUR GUILTY HANDS. And voilà! An affordable, organic, calfskin rug.

Acquire as much Midcentury Glassware as Humanly Possible

Mason jars are played out. These days it's all about drinking from vintage chemistry sets. Break into an abandoned school and steal a bunch of busted test tubes. Take home, clean well, and use the beakers as shot glasses to distribute the moonshine you made in your claw-foot tub. You can also use them as tiny vases for a floating display of foraged flora from your urban oasis/the alley behind your house.

Scandinavi-yeah!

A laut of umlauts, is what you're going for. No matter what Scandi item you have in your home, it's important that the name of the designer or object itself is impossible to discern from looking at it. Bonus points if its function and categorization are equally obscure on first glance. Is it a chair? Is it an art? Yes.

Redecorate... With Words

Describe your space carefully and everyone will be raving about the "reclaimed outdoor living area" in your "semi-converted urban greenspace" (you live in a downtown ravine), your "vintage revival kitchen" (you employ a child to clean it and there's a threat of typhoid), and the "found elements" in your bathroom (bugs). Remember: a picture is worth a thousand words, but the right words are worth a million RTs. #wise #sowise #wiseandtrue

Who Made the Art in your House?

If the answer isn't "a close personal friend, who is fantastic with mixed media and healing incantations," take it outside and burn it.

Tiny Piles

Get comfortable with the idea of everything in your home being arranged in tiny, esthetically pleasing piles. Got books? Organize them by colour, then put those colours in tiny piles! Vintage toys last played with by children long-dead? Pile 'em up! Just had a baby? Invite a few friends' babies over and STACK THOSE BABIES.

WARNING: If You Do Not Have a Prominent Reading Nook, People Will Assume You Are Illiterate

And why shouldn't they, where do you even read if not be-nooked?

Accessorize with Animals

Cool lizards, colourful fish, and tiny dogs with sad eyes are projected to be very hot for 2016 interiors. Cats, of course, are a perennially popular choice and can really spruce up a mid-century sofa. Those uninterested in animals should consider a terrarium, aka a fish tank minus the water or fish. Succulents are the preferred pet of trendy women with allergies to animal dander, though a tasteful smattering of crystals may be substituted if the homeowner truly cannot be trusted to care for a living thing.

"Upcycle" Your Friends

No offence to your friends, it's just that when it comes down to it, they don't have enough tattoos based on eighteenth-century woodcuts. When auditioning new friends try to find some or all of the following: vegans who bake, lesbians with septum piercings, bearded men with strong arms, women with Etsy stores, gay guys who live in foreign countries but bring you exquisite gifts when they're in town, a mixologist, a couple with a sex Tumblr, someone who currently works as a cartographer, people of any gender who make their own clothes, and one Basic (to prove you're nice).

NB: while these are very helpful and accurate tips, if you do not already live in Berlin, I can't really help you. *Entschuldigung, hündin!*

Facebook, I Have Some Questions

I'm confused, FB. I'm so confused.

Why do you have a popular game called "Dog Mafia" and how do I stop getting invitations to play it?
I really do not need a canine gang war right now, I'm stressed enough trying to figure out how to respond to my second cousin's misogynist photo caption.

Who do you think you're fooling with those privacy settings, though?
I see you. I'm not going to read the updated settings or log off or anything, but I see you, and I've read some articles, and I don't totally understand what's going on, but I can tell that it's bad. Probably. Almost certainly. Don't ask me for specifics, it's just bad and I know it.

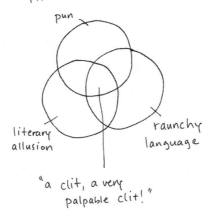

THE PERFECT SEXT

pun

literary allusion

raunchy language

"a clit, a very palpable clit!"

Should I be standing shoulder-to-shoulder with a bunch of bikini-clad women on a beach all crossing our arms behind our backs more often, or what?

From what I've gleaned, you have to do this a few times a year to stay under a certain BMI. Can you provide more information about where to meet Bikini Friends, and what beaches are ideal for crossing our arms behind our backs together looking out at the sun setting into the sea? Any help appreciated, thank you.

What do you do when your attractive colleague adds you and you accept the invite late at night and go on a wine-based stalking spree and accidentally "like" a photo from 2008?

Asking for a friend.

Where is the flattering angle detection technology we're all clamouring for?

Oh, so you can detect our faces to tag them, but you can't tell when we have a Bad Chin? This is a misuse of company funds.

The people are crying out for an end to unflattering tags. Heed their call. Someday, somewhere, someone will get a hold of those photos from the 2004 Facebook employee Christmas party, and then you'll have to listen. Act now, and no one needs to see the video of Dustin Moskovitz "getting jiggy" to Lady Gaga with some inebriated programmers.

My mom has never once shared one of those "SHARE AND LIKE THIS PHOTO IF YOU ARE PROUD OF YOUR DAUGHTER." Should I be reading into this, Y/N?

On the one hand, those are clearly bogus clickbait with no actual bearing on anyone's real, human emotions. On the other, she did share one that said, "SHARE AND LIKE IF YOU ARE PROUD OF YOUR ELDEST DAUGHTER SPECIFICALLY, LOVE YOU ALICE, YOU'RE MY EVERYTHING," so... ?

Why are you allowed to send invites to people who live in different cities than you?

Like, I'm probably not coming to your comedy show. I'm definitely not coming to your comedy show in Buffalo, NY.

Why is hatebooking still a thing?

I am not here for people who treat Facebook like a zoo of human error. Who cares how tacky that guy from your old music class is? Why do you need to look at 100 pictures of your ex's new girlfriend? You don't. This is a very common, very human, but very ugly practice that we are all guilty of engaging in more than we'd like to admit. Let's just try not to, this year, yeah? It's nice out—you have better things to do! I know That Girl just changed her status to "~*~*the truth is in the stars, and damien you are my star*~*~," but you don't know what that means and you never will! Neither does she! Move it along, nothing to see here.

Why pretend that Facebook chat is not EXCLUSIVELY for flirting?

How to tell if someone talking to you on Facebook chat is into you: they are talking to you on Facebook chat. Those invasive blue windows are like one enlarged, angular winky-face.

What's... going on, with poking, exactly?

"Facebook is a dynamic, ever-changing social media platform. As such, it's important that we're constantly updating and changing all of its features. Nothing shall remain the same, change is progr–oh, the poke function? Don't touch it. It's perfect."—Mark Zuckerberg

A Guide To Sexy Selfie Poses

❀

It's confirmed, sexting is not just for horny teens anymore (they've moved on to full anal). People of all ages, shapes, and sizes are taking and sending sexy photos of themselves, and why not?

Stress, is why not. So much stress. The whole production is an anxiety-inducing mess. What time of day do you send it? What kind of face do you make? What's The Cloud? What angle makes your boobs look most fun and symmetrical but also like "Oh, me? Just hanging out with these. VERY similar shapes. Anyway, a camera sort of materialized and I snapped a quick pic, you know? Thought I'd send your way just for a bit of titillation. Quick pun for you there. I'm very light-hearted. Anyway, I don't know why I left you a voice message about a sext, but here we go. Had a lot of fun last week!"

216

Don't panic. Next time you're staring down the barrel of your smartphone drenched in stress-sweat, pretend it's sultry Moroccan oil and bust out one of these tried-and-tested poses.

The Incognito

If you don't know someone that well, you don't know what they're going to do with this picture. A mutual right swipe on Tinder might mean shared attraction but it certainly doesn't mean a shared moral code. Don't include your face or other identifying features in a sexy picture until one or both of the following is true: a) you wouldn't care if it ended up online somewhere because, hello, you look and feel amazing, www.YOUREWELCOME. com, and/or b) you trust the person in question at least enough to presume they'd get permission before making you Internet-famous. If not, obscure your face with careful camera angles, "I'm shy" hands, jaunty accessories (large conch you got on that freshman trip to Florida? Favourite childhood stuffed animal?), or fun, mysterious masks. Looks like it was Miss. Terious, in her parents' bathroom, with the iPhone.

The Wh...at Is That?

Give your sextee a photo they'll look at over and over again... in an effort to discern what exactly it is you've sent them. The blurrier the better, here. We want an XXX-treme close-up of... something. Could be anything. Should probably be a b-hole. (Not necessarily yours! Maybe that's part of the surprise!!) An unidentifiable shadow with a caption "can't wait to do this to you" will have them thinking about you for days. Are you going to give them a massage or injure them in some way? Is this a set up? You'll never tell! ;)

The Barely Legal

Taking its cue from one of the most popular pornographic genres in the world, the goal of this selfie is to look freshly eighteen, so apply your mascara poorly, don't cover up that heavy undergrounder of a zit your chin's been brewing, and make a face that says, "I'm just discovering feminism and have read SO many articles about whether or not what I'm doing right now is cool that I honestly can't decide and all I really know is that I want you to like me." For added detail, play an earnest female singer-songwriter in the background. Your recipient won't know, but you will. Accompany your pic with a number of eggplant emojis, and send it by whatever has replaced Snapchat (I don't know what it is but I'm sure it's something).

The Mission Impossible

Set the bar incredibly high for in-person interaction by micro-managing every detail of your selfie until you have the taken the Perfect Sexy Photo. This will only take 600 or so tries. See if you can rent some studio lighting from a local photography school at a low cost, and get a friend or seven to come over and act as crew. Spend three or four months beforehand taking yoga and pilates classes to limber up, and when it comes to the big day, just be [a VERY carefully positioned, perfectly made up, flatteringly contorted version of] yourself! Then it's just a few hours in the editing suite and you're minutes away from sending an easy, breezy, sexy pic! #IWokeUpLikeThis

The Please Stop Texting Me

Is there anything in this world sadder than an unsolicited dick pic? Gentlemen, if you are reading this, please note: no woman in history has ever received an unasked-for shot of a peen and thought, "Oh, wow. He's FUN. I've really overlooked him in a sexual way for reasons of like, general compatibility and taste and the heart wanting what it wants, but now... I mean, this is a game changer. Call me Wales in springtime because I am WET!" If someone is bothering you with their dick pics, save one and edit it so their penis is just... gone. Send it back to them, then block.

The Girlfriend Experience

Pull your hair back in a scrunchie and make a face that says, "Please clean the cat's litter box, I know it's my turn but I'm tiiiiiired." Lightly pinch a boob in one hand and hold a slice of pizza in the other. Eat all remaining pizza before your significant other gets home.

You can do it! Remember: a journey of a thousand miles starts with a single sext.

Is This Important?

A Quiz for Internet Users

First of all: how do you feel?

a. Sad.

b. Angry.

c. Very Angry.

d. OUTRAGED.

Thank you for your feedback. Now, *why* do you feel that way?

a. Someone tweeted something mean about me.

b. I read a blog post that made me angry.

c. I read a response to a blog post that made me angry.

d. I wrote a response to someone's blog post response that made me so angry and then someone tweeted something mean about it.

How did you respond?

a. I have engaged them in a twenty-one Tweet-long argument and started a hashtag (#noyoushutup) so people on my side can weigh in.

b. I posted a 3,000 word Facebook status about the matter, inviting my cousins and ex-girlfriends to weigh in.

c. Emailed the writer of the response post AND the original post, telling everyone involved they should be ashamed of themselves. Called for the firing of the original piece's editor, the web manager of the site that hosted the response, and the author of the response's mother (she works as a nurse).

d. I expressed myself through the medium of gifs on Tumblr. As of my last count it has over twelve (12!) notes.

Whose fault is this?

a. Maybe Social Justice Warriors, possibly the Liberal or Conservative Media, almost certainly "elitist bloggers."

b. Probably if I go back far enough it's the fault of being bullied at a young age but at the minute I'm gonna have to say Capitalism?

c. A tie between Fast Food and "This Economy."

d. Millennials.

What are other people saying online about this?

a. "yo fuck that bitch she's a stupid feminist who should die ps what did she do #noyoushutup"—@GunsAndCheeseFries

b. "this is the stupidest thing i've ever read. honestly you're an evil person who should resign, then die"—@HelenMomOf3

c. "die die die die die die die die die"—@BonerBaby69Lol

d. "tHiS iS a CoNsPiRaCy By BiG OiL bUt AlSo I tHiNk eCo-FrEaKs BeAr SoMe BlAmE, aNyWaY, DiE."—@_human_garbage_

If you tried to explain this to your mom, she would say:
a. "What's Twatter?"
b. "Who's Gawker, you should email him."
c. "You know I think the little blogs you do are so great, keep it up! Send me a link to one some time so I can read it!"
d. "I need you to spend less time on the computer, your father and I are worried about you."

After literally hours in front of your computer dealing with this problem, you feel:
a. Sad (and tired).
b. Angry (and stressed and tired).
c. Very Angry (and worn out and tired).
d. OUTRAGED (and hungry).

Mostly A's
This is not important. It's the Internet.

Mostly B's
This is not important. It's the Internet.

Mostly C's
This is not important. It's the Internet.

Mostly D's
This is not important. It's the Internet.

A Poem About Texting

❄

look
we're all on our phones
all
the
time

i know you saw it
and you know
i know

so

i mean.

I AM YOUR PILLOW NOW.

How To Watch Literally Hours
Of TV At A Time

※

When faced with a cornucopia of deliciousness, sometimes the only thing to do is dive right in and gorge yourself. Which is why there is no greater pleasure than a lazy afternoon to do just that with a new or classic TV series. Gone are the days when you had to wait for a television show to be on at its scheduled time. When you had to watch commercials. When you had to own a TV. Suck it, Mom and Dad. Screw you, Dick and Jane. The TV of your era is gone; it's been replaced with something important: antisocial, extended bingeing. We're talking serious, marathon TV sessions. Sometimes they are on purpose, when you've excitedly cleared your schedj to really get into *Buffy*, and sometimes they are by accident, when you decide to check out what all the *Orphan Black* fuss is about, and emerge twelve hours later, riveted and trying on different fun accents and wondering if you could pull off dreadlocks. So, what are the best circumstances under which to consume eight straight episodes of *30 Rock*, an entire season of *The Wire* or every *Arrested Development* blooper reel in existence? Let's discuss.

If You Gonna Do the Crime (show), You Gotta Have the Time

"I got sucked into a TV hole" is one of the scummiest excuses for bailing out that there is, so try to schedule your *Golden Girls* marathon during a life moment where you've got between three and seventeen spare hours at the ready. Top times include: post-break up, that period of a new relationship where all you guys wanna do is hang out alone, one of those super gross cold weekends after Christmas where no one is going out anyway because we're all brooooooke, or late at night when you have a book deadline looming over your head but you're feeling reckless and really loving seeing Pryzbylewski flourish as a teacher.

Know What You're Getting Yourself Into

The thing about binge TV consumption is that a television show traverses a lot of emotional ground over the course of an entire season. Theoretically, this is parsed out over weeks, with time to digest and think about what you've seen, but if you're getting all PVR-gluttonous about it, this might be a pretty intense ride, feelings-wise. Are you ready to get to know some characters, fall in love with them, learn about their hopes and dreams, watch them fail and succeed, and then watch them HAVE THEIR THROAT SLIT WHILE THEIR FAMILY DIES AROUND THEM?? *Jesus, Game of Thrones*. Jesus and all seven gods. Ask yourself if you can handle that, emotionally, because a lot of good television is extremely heart-wrenching, and that shit can get to you. A full day of *Homeland* = a full day of stress diarrhea. A full night of *Dexter* = a full night of staying up until it's light out because you're not scared, but also there is probably a serial killer in your bathroom, best just to hold it. Are you sure you don't just want to watch *Spaced* again? Maybe just watch *Spaced* again.

Pack Smart

You're going on a journey. An odyssey of the mind. A test of endurance for your brain, emotions, and bladder. Figure out in advance what provisions you will need, and this includes viewing company. No offence to humans, but pets are the ideal companion for this kind of thing. They do not talk too much but are capable of providing the requisite comfort required during more difficult moments. Plus, purring. What a great feature. As for snacks, these should be shareable in case of human companions, and probably crunchy? I'm just spitballing here. (Don't eat anything that could end up a spitball.) Also know what you're in the mood for, i.e. nothing with ghosts if you are home alone (this is a good tip for everyone and not just something I learned the hard way), nothing super lovey-dovey if you have been recently dumped, no intense medical dramas if you've just spent a bunch of crappy time in a hospital… you get it.

Size Matters

A crucial joy of the binge is that it stretches for hours and hours, an all-you-can-eat buffet for the eyes. Obviously it will be a short gorge if the show only has three episodes to-date. Programming that ended in its prime is ideal here, which is why the BBC and British programming in general is your friend. American television has a tendency to run much-loved shows into the ground by refusing to ever say die; Canadian television looks like it could turn into low-budget porn at any moment. The best of British TV is well-crafted drama and comedy that knows to end on a high note (plus lots of soft-looking men in sweaters with accents). Which is great, because six seasons is more work than you can do in a weekend; faced with the entire œuvre of the American *Office* you might just give up, get off the couch and go outside, and who wants that? The UK *Office* will sort you right out, with fourteen well-crafted episodes that you can devour in one or two committed sittings. *Arrested Development*'s original series is also ideal TV binge material. Fire up the Netflix but maybe quit while you're ahead at season three. No tea, some shade: season four bums me out (cue Charlie Brown music, entire cast exits with its head hung sadly, Ann remains and eats a whole egg in one go. *Fin*).

Do Not Give In to the Allure of the Outside World

There will be social events. There will be the urge, maybe, to get some physical activity. Once you are ensconced in the sweet, pillow-y comfort of your bed area, wriggle in tight and don't get out. Our puritan ancestors have ruined a lot of things for us, including but not limited to: hats, sex, alcohol, and how we view leisure. Not working for a day or two is not the worst thing in the world. We all work all the damn time. Taking a second to just full-on, unashamedly veg is both A-OK and probably good for your health in the long run. I am sure a doctor somewhere is reading this right now and nodding: "Good science, Monica. This whole piece clearly demonstrates your medical prowess and general grownup life skills, now get back into bed!"—that doctor.

Thank you, Dr. Science. I rest my case.

A Final Word of Warning:

OnDemand viewing can ruin you. It is the My Mom's Cheesecake* of entertainment—once you've had it you don't want to eat cheesecake any other way ever again. I started watching *Mad Men* several years late, caught up, and now have given up on the series for a while because I literally can't bear to wait six days for more updates on what Joan and the gang are doing, what a spoiled brat I am.

Join me, fellow brats. Fire up those laptops, give up on seeing daylight today, slip into a Snuggie (RIP), and get ready to leave your butt imprints on the couch. Happy viewing!

*(vehemently not a euphemism)

A Day In The Life Of Pinterest

✤

The sun shines through Pinterest's upcycled stained glass window, catching the mirrored elements on the mobile she crafted with her mother. Pinterest stirs underneath a quilt made of old T-shirts, a clever #lifehack that allows her to incorporate cherished memories of her past into the cozy comfort of her future. She looks at the ceiling. *Breathe*, it says. She does. Today feels like a gift. "I guess that's why they call it the present," she thinks to herself. She water colours the phrase on an antique book and leaves it on the crafts rack to dry.

Getting out of her cast-iron vintage bed, Pinterest nearly trips on a pile of antlers. Whoops! She must have been arranging wall clusters in her sleep again. She puts the antlers back where they belong—on the head of the live deer that hangs out by her window. She puts a flower crown on the deer and feeds it some homemade maca-and-almond energy balls before it scuttles off to explore the farmland surrounding the property. "Cherish each moment!!!" she yells after it. She shakes a few stray thoughts out of the dreamcatcher gifted to her by her grandmother, then slips her feet into some carbon-neutral rice-paper sandals she bought in Japan.

Pinterest's day begins with a ritual thanking of the universe for its bounty, plus wonderment at how quickly you can turn cashews from humble nuts into a rich, creamy dressing. "Gratitude and humility," she reminds her family of terrariums. "And dedication to the mission." The succulents look back at her knowingly. They get it. She looks to her Motivation Wall and picks out the day's themes: power, strength, ombre accents. She throws a few darts at the picture of Gwyneth Paltrow she keeps taped to the inside of her market-scavenged medical cabinet. "There can only be one," she whispers softly, slathering her face and body with a coconut oil scrub. She gets the most out of her mascara by pouring some contact lens solution into the old tube. Pinterest is thrifty.

All this skincare has made her hungry for thoughtfully prepared, hearty food. "Hail Seitan," she mutters to herself, rummaging through jars of preserves, wrapped up mug-cakes, and gluten-free farm-to-table sustainable almond butter. Suddenly she remembers: overnight oats! The taste of chia seeds, organic raspberry compote, and whole oats feel healing; it gives her energy. "Suck on that, Blake Lively," she says between gulps. The oats are gone in less than thirty seconds. Thank God for cheat days! Pinterest's tattoo (many small birds in the shape of a larger bird) peeks out of her sleeve as she does the dishes in a bucket she found on a shipwreck.

Thinking about Blake has Pinterest revved up. She tries to do some delicate felting, but instead stabs her knitting needles into the wheel of her fixie. "Darn," she says, immediately regretting the curse word and feeling like a traitor to the bicycle rights cause. She quickly and expertly mends the wheel using only spices. She takes down a few reams of burlap and makes a nest in the living room. Pinterest feels safe in the nest. Calm. She paints little garden scenes on each of her nails and does a few hours of glitter crafts. Did you know you can turn regular pinecones into gold-covered pinecones with the simple addition of some gold?

After a lunch of raw quinoa eaten near a waterfall, she heads to her special place. Pinterest spends every day from 11 AM to 5 PM trying on *very* casual wedding dresses in a secret room, drunk on herb-infused signature cocktails. She eats raw vegan canapés and sings Beyoncé lyrics while pasting pictures of herself holding various quirky props (moustaches!!!!) into scrapbooks. She has thousands and thousands of scrapbooks. They are organized by the colour of their spines, to pleasing effect. One day, she knows, she will have a wedding. One day, she will feel whole.

Back in her kitchen, she starts the evening's work: repurposing things. She repurposes a chandelier into a centrepiece, an unwanted blanket into a whimsical teepee, a large can into a slightly smaller can. It feels good to recycle. "Come at me, Martha Stewart. I freaking dare you," Pinterest thinks as she paints the final chevron on what used to be a useless old ladder. Now it's a cool ladder. She lights a match and illuminates a few homemade beeswax tapers. She takes one to her outdoor fire pit and ritualistically burns many copies of *House & Garden*. The light flickers across the metallic temporary tattoos she's applied along her collarbone as a fun, affordable twist on glitzy jewellery.

Hours later, there is nothing else to repurpose. Surrounded by things that have now become Beautiful Things, Pinterest feels alone. Shyly, she opens the display case where she keeps her skull art and apothecary jars. She grabs a vintage teacup and throws it on the ground. "OOOOOOOPRAH!!!!!" she yells, her eyes wild. She gathers the remains of the teacup into a tidy line and snorts it. There it is. She's having one of her nights now. This is how it has to be. She runs through the house, grabbing a ceramic fox. She breaks it and her hungry nostrils snort the pieces up greedily. She rolls up the pages of the 1916 edition of *Alice In Wonderland* and smokes them, just to feel something. She stacks old milk crates on Coke crates on vintage trunks and jumps into a pile of faux fur throws. She feels more alive than the time she painted the vestibule an unexpectedly bright accent colour. She keeps at it all night, smoking and snorting curios and tchotchkes, mainlining fair-trade coffee, huffing Washi tape, and stencilling thank-you cards to her guests. She passes out with one hand holding a lighter to a spoon full of coral she'd found on a trip to the Bahamas.

Pinterest sleeps fitfully on the exposed-brick ground, surrounded by broken glass, spilled glue, and shadowboxes full of taxidermied butterflies. Tomorrow she'll wake up and feel immediate regret. She'll clean the house with apple cider vinegar and start a cleanse. She'll wonder how it all went so wrong. She'll throw a few more darts than usual at Gwyneth Paltrow. But that's tomorrow. For now, she sleeps. In the dark, a neon sign glows: KEEP CALM AND CARRY ON.

Acknowledgments

Whew. Okay. I am a very lucky person with many people to thank and if I mess this up and forget someone please know I am very grateful, but also if an omission like that can happen to Hilary Swank it can happen to anyone.

Most important thanks are to my family—Alice, Mel, Mom, Dad, Sadie, Boots—for putting up with me for twenty-six years and for their kindness, wit, and love. Also to Alex's family, who are becoming mine, for the same during a shorter time-frame. Your support and generosity (of spirit and of money, so much money over so many years my god) means so much to me and I am lucky and grateful to have you in my life.

I'd also like to thank Carly Watters and P.S. Literary for guiding me gently through the process of making this thing, Richard Dionne for coming up with the idea in the first place, Natasha Tsakiris for being so sweet and helpful and enthusiastic, and everyone at Red Deer Press for agreeing to print my words on paper and bind them together. Very extreme thanks to young genius Jenn Kitagawa for the cover art, to Paul Terefenko for a lovely author photo, and to Charles Yao for being a hero in many ways, cover and otherwise. I am also indebted to the representation and wise counsel of Lauren Smythe at InkWell Management.

A million thanks also to Lena Dunham, Rob Delaney, Tabatha Southey, Katie Heaney, and Amy Rose Spiegel for their kind words

about the book and for helping in my ongoing quest to convince my little sister's friends that I am cool.

About 30% of the material in this book originally appeared on shedoesthecity.com; many thanks are due to Jen McNeely for running my work in the first place, and for her encouragement and support with this project.

A few people were very crucial to the editing process of this book: Richard, obviously, who edited patiently and let me make so many boner jokes and acted like they were very normal jokes an adult author would make; Kathleen Hale, kind soul and first living human to see a full draft; Hali Hamilton, my always-editor and the best G-chat based content consultant in the biz; Alex, always, for making me funnier and smarter and never ignoring the question "is this anything?" Mostly though I would like to thank Night Wine, source of most of the words in this volume.

There is also a much too long list of individual people who provided help in the form of line edits, cups of coffee, Facebook chats and welcome distractions, including but not limited to two Emilys and two Adams (the loves of my life), Travis (the MPG@Q), Jane, Haley, Anne, Hali, Allana, another Haley, another Emily, and the entire Toronto coven. Thank you to Drew for letting me be very whiny a lot of the time. I am required by Nerd Law to thank Christopher Berwick for being the kind of magical English teacher that actually changes lives.

And, no one be mad, but I have to thank Twitter. It is so full of people who make me laugh and think and who write things I just live for. The Internet is a lot of things (bad, huge, full of trolls, so bad) but it can also be pretty wonderful. It is at the very least what brought me to the websites and editors of those websites I most need to thank: Haley and Jazmine at *The Hairpin* and Alex, Kev, Jamie and Eleanor at *VICE*. I am grateful to work for you guys and hope to do more of it.

My biggest thanks are owed to Alex Tindal for basically everything.

Praise for Monica Heisey's, *I Can't Believe It's Not Better*

"It is the only humor book I ever want to own and it made me keel over with laughter and recognition. Monica Heisey's book is a perfect entry into my favorite genre: books of dubious advice. From how to eat to what to wear to who to screw, Monica attempts to offer solutions but instead reveals more about her own unique pathos— and I wouldn't want it any other way. I truly wish she could be America's poet laureate. Too bad she's Canadian." —**Lena Dunham**

"Monica Heisey makes me laugh hard and often. We could dissect her to find out why she's so funny but that would mean she'd be dead. I say "No" to that idea. But I say "Ha ha" to Monica. Often."
                          —**Rob Delaney, comedian and actor**

"Discovering Monica Heisey's work was like going to a party alone, spotting a stranger girl in a Bart Simpson T-shirt and a devastating ponytail by the donuts table, thinking, "Oh, thank God—my friend is here," and knocking over every single Solo cup in that place as you barge over with your hand outstretched. She makes a less-than-gentle and kind world seem camaraderie-stuffed and loving, and she's funny as fuck, too. Get this book inside your life."
                          —**Amy Rose Spiegel, *ROOKIE***

"Monica Heisey… is the funniest woman in America, which is amazing because she lives in Canada."
                  —**Jazmine Hughes, contributing editor of *The Hairpin***

"Monica Heisey's writing is clever, funny, and pointed, and I love how evidently and sincerely she cares about all her book's subjects, be they big (female friendship) or small (chip dips). Prepare to be moved to tears by her ode to cheese and her love letter to pizza."
                          —**Katie Heaney, author of *Never Have I Ever***